13 INSPIR

13
INSPIRATIONS

The Guiding Lights of Rugby League

Rugby League Cares

Scratching Shed Publishing Ltd

In memory of
David Gronow

Rugby League Cares

Supporting the Rugby League family & its community

Grants

Welfare

Heritage

Benevolent Fund

Enhancing and enriching people's lives through the power and positive influence of Rugby League.

Please show your support and become a member today for £20 per annum or £2 per month and receive your exclusive member gift!

For more information or to sign up visit:

www.rugbyleaguecares.org

Grants   Welfare   Heritage   Benevolent F

Gameplan

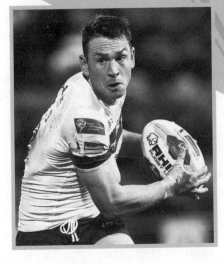

From Oldham to Old Trafford

Kevin Sinfield MBE

WHAT inspired me to play rugby league was my elder brother Ian; I wanted to be like him. Having the opportunity to run in his footsteps on a wet and muddy field in Oldham, and come home from training all dirty and not get into trouble for it, meant that I fell in love with the sport pretty quickly.

I was also able to make a load of new friends, as we faced the tackle bags and shields together, and very quickly it was all I wanted to do to have fun and keep fit.

When you get a bit older, you begin to understand the core values that have fashioned rugby league into what it is and remains; those of honesty, trust, hard work, integrity and looking out for your mate. They fitted into the kind of belief systems that I grew up with at home and have, hopefully, inherited and passed on through my family.

Along my journey, I've come across so many people who were inspirational, the bulk of whom - like school teachers and junior coaches - are volunteers but left a huge life-changing mark; people who play a massive part in your development yet don't even realise it.

What my parents were prepared to do to enable me to pursue my dream was awe-inspiring and I had an older brother and sister who looked out for me as well. It's a whole host of people who put a lot of time and effort and love and care into how you mature and grow who have such an influence. We come across those sorts of people in our lives who do things for the right, selfless reasons; for the betterment of others.

In terms of an event that made me want to be a professional player, being selected to play at Wembley in 1992 as a schoolboy representing the town and meeting the great Wigan team the day before the cup final at the stadium left a massive impression.

Likewise, spending time with the Castleford lads after they'd been beaten and a bunch of 11-year-olds pestered them for autographs, you don't forget those magical moments.

Seeing people like Ellery Hanley play to such a high standard and the way he led his men also left an indelible mark on me during those years. Some of the things he did for England and Great Britain were the very definition of inspirational. We all have heroes in the game and he was mine.

I've been fortunate to play for some brilliant coaches. You take a little bit from all of them, they have different skills and ways of working and all were good people. I've learned from each and every one. They have had a considerable impact on what we have achieved as a group and, as importantly, in our everyday lives although, again, they seldom realise it and don't get enough credit for that side.

How they prepare you, talk to you and invigorate you, especially before the big games, inspires you to go out and give your all.

I have been alongside some all-time greats on the pitch who, without a shadow of a doubt, cannot fail to leave a mark. At Leeds, the likes of Iestyn Harris, Marc Glanville, Barrie McDermott, Adrian Morley, Terry Newton, Dave Furner ... the list is long and distinguished. Every time you go out, you take a little bit of everyone you have played with out there with you and that is quite comforting, especially when the going is at its toughest.

Among the current group, I've been really fortunate to work every day alongside such as Jamie Peacock, Jamie Jones-Buchanan, Rob Burrow, Danny McGuire - I could keep reeling them off. International-wise, such as Andy Farrell, Paul Sculthorpe and Keiron Cunningham are terrific servants in their own right and you can't fail to be inspired by being around them, for different reasons.

Some of our shared memories are absolutely priceless.

There are different ways of being a captain. Some do it by word, others through deed. I see myself as a little of both, somewhere in between, certainly not a Churchill by any stretch but maybe not a JP either, who leads from the front by his actions and the way he conducts himself in the vanguard of the battle. The way he is prepared to do the tough stuff sets a phenomenal lead for all.

I'm very aware of the support I've had as skipper from the leaders in the team and the senior group and been only too happy to embrace their input and let them take the lead whenever the situation suits; it's all about giving the group maximum strength and direction. I'm extremely thankful to play alongside some special people every week.

Even as you come towards the end of your playing career, you don't think about the effect you might have on youngsters, flattering though the idea is. We realise that how we conduct ourselves and behave is important in setting the right example for the next generation.

All I try and be is the best I can be every day and as good a person as possible. If that inspires somebody else to take up our sport or make the right decision in their life, then fantastic, that is something I would be very proud of.

I'm a great believer that we have to do all we can to help those who are the unsung heroes of our sport, which is why I was so keen to support Rugby League Cares and the objectives it stands for. The selfless pioneers and deeds recorded in this brilliant book are the true essence of that.

KEVIN SINFIELD, MBE
November 2014

A Game Fit for Heroes

Tony Hannan

HUMAN beings have always loved stories … telling them, hearing them, reading them too.

It accounts for our tendency to mythologise, whether in admiring the impressive feats of others or perhaps those of ourselves or the forebears of the groups with which we feel an affinity. Stories are how we shape our individual and collective identities, and they are how we try to bring sense, order and narrative to a big bad scarily random universe.

Nowhere is that more obvious than in our behaviour around sport. Moral positions are very often adopted on the hoof and - even with more considered reflection - established according to the framework of whichever club or country we happen to support. We like to kid ourselves that our response to bad behaviour or ill-fortune is rational and fair, but it very seldom is. Family comes first, then community - religious, geographical or shared interest - and finally nation, when we are identifying good guys, bad guys, heroes and villains. We Earthlings would need to be invaded by Mars before every race and creed on the planet came together as one.

And given how most rugby league fans are *homo sapiens* themselves, it is behaviour from which the self-styled Greatest Game is far from immune. This, as we never tire of telling ourselves and any unbeliever who will listen, is the sporting world's best kept secret, brim full of top quality athletes who never quite get the acclaim they deserve. Nowhere is there a sport that makes such demands not only on the bodies of participants, but upon their minds and stamina and reserves of courage. This indomitable game, born out of injustice and discrimination at every historical turn, has stood its corner come what may, giving lie to predictions of its demise made regularly since those far-sighted northern rebels first stepped over the threshold of Huddersfield's George Hotel, way back in 1895.

There's truth in all of that, of course - as a league nut myself, I'd be bound to say so, wouldn't I? But what such broad-brush mantras also carry is a hint of self-righteousness and the myth-making instinct as described. They skirt inconvenient and more troublesome details, generalise in our favour, ignore any fact but that which paints our sport - and by extension ourselves - in all but the most flattering light.

We don't need to pick all of that apart here, although keen readers-between-the-lines will note in the forthcoming chapters any number of instances that might in any other walk of life elicit outright disapproval rather than respect or mute acceptance, a shake of the head rather than a cheer to the Gods of the version of rugby that *we* know they actually *do* play in heaven. We come to praise league, not to bury it, but as the sign outside Odsal used to say: Beware of the Bull.

It *is* a cast-iron fact, mind, that anyone who ever pulled on or pulls on a pair of rugby league boots exhibits bravery beyond the call of normal sporting duty. This is not a sport in which to hide or take an on-field breather. Life-changing danger, as the story of Matt King makes tragically clear, is an ever present, lurking in every seemingly innocuous tackle.

Similarly, myths can travel in the opposite direction, imposed - often unfairly, or even malignly - from outside. Rugby league is a simple game for simple people. Five drives and a kick. Wriggling in the mud. Northern and working class. M62 corridor *et al*. Well, again, although such accusations - we've all heard them, I'm sure - may well have contained the odd historical grain of truth, as uncomfortable as that may be to admit, happily there is much to refute such ill-informed over-generalisations in the tales to come also.

Few sports have been as entwined with community values as rugby league. And again it has been a two-way process. For while the people of towns and cities like Wigan, Sydney, Perpignan and Port Moresby have sustained the sport through good times and bad, rugby league or rugby à treize or footy, call it what you will, has very much returned the favour, bringing unity and meaning, even a way to earn a living, to the most impoverished of lives. In less dramatic circumstances, armies of unpaid volunteers - junior coaches, groundsmen, barstaff, kit washers, harassed mums and dads - have kept the game going, most often just for the love of it (or perhaps, on occasion, the love of their children).

Yet if everyone is a hero, is anyone a hero? If feats of astonishing toughness, skill and bravery happen every week, then the extraordinary, by definition, is ordinary. Amazing is par for the course. The flip side of community values can be a certain parochialism, an urge to hold people back, a distrust of individuality and ambition, tall poppy syndrome, 'who does he/she think they are?', victimhood and complacency. Another way of seeing it, of course, is that community instills a philosophy of teamwork and helps to keep people grounded.

Greatness, though, *can* be achieved and it is to those who attain it that we lesser mortals look for inspiration. You are about to re-encounter 13 such figures - a handy number - in these pages. Yet if you were able to speak to any of them, just about every one would deny their own status as a role model or exceptional character in any way. Indeed, humility is implicit in just about their every word, another readily recognisable trait among the rugby league fraternity.

So it was that when the idea for this book was first mooted by RL Cares - a fine practical charity in the very best rugby league tradition - via BBC commentator Dave Woods and the organisation's general manager Chris Rostron, two immediate tasks presented themselves.

One: ensuring that the *13 Inspirations* in question were worthy of that acclaim. They didn't need to be superstars, but they ought to be truly inspirational. The real McCoy. No need to big anyone up. No need for hype or sentimentality. Just honest to goodness rugby league people who metaphorically stood up to be counted when it really mattered, more than did their bit and inspired others to do likewise.

And two: to decide which 13 people most obviously fitted that bill. Much coffee was consumed.

As a starting point, we discussed choosing a 'top 13' - ie the 13 *greatest* inspirations - but soon dismissed that as impractical. For a start, humanity's love of mythology aside, there were just too many genuinely inspirational figures in the running and, for a finish, how can one achievement be judged 'better' than another? No, that wouldn't do at all. So the format, once it was settled, came down to one set of criteria. These are simply *13 Inspirations* as chosen by our willing bunch of writers and Rugby League Cares. They are *not* the definitive 13 by any means. It would be a major surprise if every single reader of this book did not have an alternative 13 of their own and part of the reasoning behind it is we hope it will spark what used to be called 'tap room discussion'. These days you can no doubt debate it online.

Assuming this first edition is successful and sells in sufficient quantities, with profits going back into the rugby league community via RL Cares, it is also envisaged that there may be a volume two, or even three, four, five and beyond. There are certainly more than enough candidates, many of whom play cameos in the stories already published here.

One thing is for sure, the 13 fine individuals who did make the list - along with Kevin Sinfield MBE, contributor of our foreword - are more than worthy of inclusion. Whether it's Douglas Clark, hero of Rorke's Drift and more, risking life and limb on the World War One battlefields, Mike Gregory and Steve Prescott staring death in the eye and then some, or long-serving veterans like Jamie Peacock and Adrian Morley inspiring young and old with feats on the field as well as off it, few could seriously doubt that.

Some such as Kay Ibbetson and Cec Thompson raise interesting points as to the nature of league's place within wider society. The latter was the first black Englishman to play for Great Britain, but while league likes to pride itself on historic inclusivity, how much of that was down to altruism and how much no-nonsense commercial acumen, with a view to getting the biggest talents on the field whatever their colour or cultural background, the better to maximise gate receipts? Despite Ibbetson's admirable pioneering work, to what extent was women's rugby league ever likely to reach full bloom in a society that, until the 2012 Olympics it seems, valued women's sport so lightly and in a sport so obviously marginalised, we might even say *ghetto*-ised, beyond that?

Similarly, in the famous story of the Battle of Brisbane and the role of the great Alan Prescott within it, the man himself describes playing 77 minutes with a broken arm as 'silly'. We should admire such bravery and devotion absolutely - who wouldn't follow such a selfless and downright gutsy leader, out of the trenches? But don't such adventures also inspire thoughts about just what it is that we expect from our athletes whenever we cheer them onto - or more pertinently boo them *from* - the field, even allowing for a modern-day 'duty of care'? As recently as 2014, with South Sydney Rabbitohs, Sam Burgess played through almost an entire NRL Grand Final in Sydney with a fractured cheekbone and eye socket en route to winning the Clive Churchill medal as man of the match. In and amidst all the glory, there is plenty to mull over in this book for readers who enjoy a challenging subtext too.

Ultimately, what these 13 stories prove, if proof were needed, is that rugby league is a multi-faceted character-building sport of endless contradictions that has asked much of all who have played, watched, photographed, administrated, officiated, coached, commentated on or written about it, most often with little wider recognition in the face of heavy odds. But, boy, has it delivered. And we do it because we love it.

Here be myths and legends. Prepare to be inspired.

1. Bringing It All Back Home

Gareth Walker

YOU would hesitate to say he has 'feet of clay' - not within earshot anyway, he is 6ft 3in tall and weighs 16.7 stone - but there is something very 'rugby league' about the inspirational qualities of Adrian Morley.

Fiercely proud of his working class roots, humble despite his celebrity status, Morley is universally admired by all who know him. And although he does indeed have his flaws, few sporting icons have been as publicly honest about their failings as the man they call 'Moz'. He has never shied away from his indiscretions, on or off the field.

The prologue to his excellent autobiography - also called *Moz* - charts first his record 12-second dismissal for

Great Britain against Australia in 2003, and then an ensuing run-in with police that saw him chased by dogs after being caught drink driving and CS gassed. He then gave a false name to the officers. Part-way through that story he smashes through the panel of a garden fence - as he has done with opposition defences for two decades - and when the owner opens the curtains to see what the commotion is, Morley mouths the word 'sorry'. There's plenty of the loveable rogue in Adrian Morley.

But his on-field achievements cannot be questioned. A promising young player with his local club Eccles, he was often overshadowed as a junior by his teammate Nathan McAvoy. Both were courted by several professional sides, but while Salford offered McAvoy a contract, Morley was left disappointed, ignored by the team he grew up supporting. Until, that is, Leeds boss Doug Laughton turned up in his front room, accepted two of his father's cigarettes and offered them more than any of the family had imagined to sign on the dotted line at Headingley.

From there Morley's remarkable rugby league story unfolded. Still a trainee electrician, he made his first team debut at the age of 17 alongside a man he himself had grown up idolising, Ellery Hanley, even if they were only on the same pitch for a matter of five minutes or so. Morley quickly established himself as one of the country's most destructive second-rowers, terrorising defences and earning call-ups for England and Great Britain in 1996. Three years later he was a part of the Leeds Rhinos side that ended a 21-year drought by lifting the Challenge Cup, beating London Broncos 52-16 at Wembley.

Then came the next, arguably defining chapter of his career. Before the current era when Englishmen are less rare in the much fêted NRL, Morley joined Sydney Roosters. It had been decades since an Australian club had signed such a high profile player from these shores and media scrutiny was intense from the start. It took Morley at least 12 months to fully adapt to the switch.

But after that, the Roosters fans took him firmly to their hearts, and the big-hitting Englishman became a key part of an extended period of success. Morley helped them to three consecutive NRL Grand Finals, the first of which they won in 2002, ending their own 27-year wait for a title.

They lost the following two, but Morley was very much a local hero on Bondi Beach, despite racking up a host of suspensions during his time there. Australian supporters are not renowned for singing at matches, but such was Morley's standing in the eastern suburbs that he inspired the following ditty to the Dean Martin tune, 'That's Amore':

> When you're down on your ass,
> with a face full of grass,
> that's a Morley.

While in Sydney, he added another honour to his list when he won the 2003 World Club Challenge by beating St Helens 38-0, even scoring a rare try himself.

Morley was still a Rooster when he then became the first, and still only Englishman to complete the treble of Grand Final wins on both sides of the world, plus a Challenge Cup. Morley was signed on a short-term deal by Bradford coach Brian Noble in 2005, and played in the Bulls' Grand Final win over Leeds Rhinos at Old Trafford.

That was a prelude to him returning to England permanently following the 2006 NRL season. Morley signed a four-year contract with ambitious Warrington, and became their marquee player following the move from Wilderspool to the Halliwell Jones Stadium. Again, it didn't start well. The man mountain shattered his cheekbone 37 minutes into his Warrington debut when he collided with Wigan prop Eamon O'Carroll, and after 11 weeks out he broke it again on his return.

But after that, Morley became one of the pillars on which Warrington's recent rise to prominence has been built. He lifted the Challenge Cup with the Wolves in 2009, 2010 and 2012, and was also a member of the side that reached two Grand Finals, losing in 2012 and 2013.

And finally, he fulfilled a long-held ambition to sign for the side that had overlooked him as a youngster, Salford, when he became one of the biggest names in the club's self-proclaimed 'Red Devilution' rebirth. And while, at the time of writing, the Red Devils have not yet hit the heights expected despite significant financial input from extrovert billionaire owner Dr Marwan Koukash, Morley has been a constant rock up front, producing displays that have belied his age and led to talk of one more Super League season.

Throughout all of this, perhaps the most important element of Morley's playing career has been the manner in which he has represented his country. Capped a record 53 times in total by Great Britain and England, he skippered the Lions against France in 2007 and was due to captain England in the 2010 Four Nations before sustaining an injury in the warm-up against New Zealand Maori.

And while that 12-second dismissal against Australia in 2003 might remain his most iconic contribution in his country's shirt - in which Robbie Kearns was clattered around the chops from the kick-off and British referee Steve Ganson brandished an instant red card - it should not overshadow his performances in the other 52 matches, when he led his side from the front, most often against the odds.

Like any hero, Morley has endured his fair share of adversity as well. Aged 13, he sustained a shoulder injury that resulted in a nerve problem in his left arm. It almost cost him his first professional contract - fortunately Laughton believed that if he could play that well with a bad arm, he'd be outstanding when fit - and it restricted his movement throughout his career.

During his time with Warrington, he first suffered two broken cheekbones, and then suffered regularly from double vision - a problem that threatened to end his career prematurely until a surgeon from Liverpool managed to rectify it. But perhaps the real measure of Morley, both as a player and a person, comes from his peers.

Do a quick internet search for his name and there are no lack of ringing endorsements. Tony Smith, Ellery Hanley, even Manchester United great Ryan Giggs line up to sing his praises. Among them is his former Sydney Roosters coach Ricky Stuart.

Speaking in 2006, when Morley was facing Stuart's Australian side with Great Britain in the Tri-Nations, the ex-Kangaroos scrum-half nailed much of the essence of Morley.

'In my term as an NRL coach, he will go down as one of my favourite players,' Stuart said. 'Moz is a man. He takes responsibility and makes sacrifices for the team. He does everything at 100 per cent. I have a motto as coach that I want players in my side who other players want to play alongside. And everyone wants to play alongside Moz.'

Nor when *Wigan Observer* sports editor Phil Wilkinson sat down to write Morley's autobiography, was he short of people willing to provide glowing tributes, including Stuart himself. Here are a few snapshots of others.

Manchester United legend Giggs - a fellow Salfordian - wrote in the introduction: 'Not many British players have been out to Australia and made the same impact he has. Adrian was and is regarded as one of the world's top players and in the area where we grew up, people are extremely proud of him and rightly so. We live less than a mile apart, and away from the pitch he's a terrific fella. He's always willing to help others. A few years ago, a local rugby union player broke his neck. When his mates rallied round, Moz was there to lend his hand. That's the kind of bloke he is.'

Morley's own hero Hanley was another to sing his praises. Hanley said: 'I only ever played alongside Adrian for a few minutes, but I saw enough of him then to convince me he was destined to be a great player. Journalists and broadcasters write and say nice things about Adrian, but if you really want to know how good he is, speak to the players, his team-mates, his opponents. The amount of respect they have for him is immeasurable. That tells you everything.'

One of those team-mates - and opponents - was another who figures in this book, Jamie Peacock. He wrote: 'Each week, fans get an 80-minute snapshot into what rugby league players are like. But the impression they probably get of Adrian Morley could not be further from the truth. Because that same, aggressive, confrontational forward who has inflicted so much pain on so many, for so many years, is possibly one of the nicest people you could ever wish to meet. He never gives an inch on the field, but is so kind off it. Everyone likes Moz. Players can't speak highly enough of him, even the blokes he's whacked high - and he's whacked quite a few!'

Among that list is former New Zealand skipper and centre-turned prop Ruben Wiki, but he was another to contribute to the book.

'I've few regrets from my career, but I'm pretty gutted I never got the chance to play alongside Adrian Morley,' Wiki offered. 'That would have been awesome, because I have so much respect for him, firstly as a person and then a player. The best gift you can give is your time, and that is something Moz will always give to you.'

Author Wilkinson got to know Morley better than most during the year he spent writing his autobiography. Working for extended periods alongside sportsmen at the top of their game cannot always be an easy experience for journalists, but Wilkinson had no such problems with his subject. 'Adrian Morley is a paradox,' he says. 'Rarely has a bloke whacked so many players and been so absurdly popular with, well, everyone. Everyone loves Moz.

'That was confirmed to me when I spent the better-part, the best part, of a year ghost-writing his autobiography. When he infamously got red-carded for his high-shot on Kearns, the Kangaroos players didn't seek revenge or retribution - they invited him on a night out. When his hugely successful spell with Sydney Roosters was cut short by suspension, his opponents wrote to the disciplinary panel to plead for leniency. Heck, his friendship with Ruben Wiki was forged in a hospital waiting room - and Moz was the one who put him there!

'Why do they love him so much? Because he has integrity. Honesty. And when the full-time whistle has gone, a permanent smile on his face.

'His popularity is boundless. Walk with him into a Starbucks or a McDonalds or a pub anywhere in rugby league-land, and it's like accompanying Austin Powers, as people turn to speak to him and ask him how he's doing. And he asks them back. Whether it's selfies or signing a shirt, charities or just a chat, he finds time for everyone. Nothing is too much trouble.

'That partly explains why fans love him. And the

other part? Well, that's to do with the path he took to the top. He was the working-class kid who refused to give up. He even worked as an apprentice electrician on the same day he made his Leeds debut [in an era when 'Leeds' and 'Rhinos' went together like curry and custard]. He not only beat the Aussies, he joined them, trailing a blaze in the modern era for Gareth Ellis, Brian Carney, James Graham, Sam Burgess and Sam Tomkins to follow.

'And he continues to inspire, proving age is just a number. His name often pops up when players are asked to name their toughest opponents. Ask those same players who they respect the most, who they like the most, who inspired them the most, and I'm sure many would reply with the same three-letter word - Moz.'

Another man who got to know Morley up close is Paul Cullen. He was Warrington coach when the fiercely ambitious Wolves were after a signing that would turn heads towards the end of 2006. The club had by then moved away from their spiritual home at Wilderspool to the plush new Halliwell Jones Stadium, but while that unquestionably ushered in a new era, the rebuild was far from complete and Warrington were not yet challenging seriously for trophies.

Cullen identified Morley - at the peak of his powers in Australia at the time - as the man who could help change all of that.

'Adrian Morley's recruitment was a very considered process, a real holistic approach,' Cullen explained. 'We needed somebody who was more than just an international prop forward, more than just a high-profile signing and more than just an addition to change what we were doing to improve the culture at Warrington. To find somebody who could tick so many boxes took a very thorough and serious approach.

'We were also looking to make a statement about where we were as a club. Previously, we'd been rebuilding a team and didn't have time and budgets to address so many issues. I'd needed players that could come in and do a job with immediate effect. But by then we were a few seasons into that rebuild, we had left Wilderspool, arrived at the HJ successfully and we were changing the club from the bottom upwards and from inside-out. The signing had to fill seats as well as improve the culture of the club for the better, and as a coach he had to provide me with a on-field weapon that nobody else had.'

There aren't many players like that around, in any era. But in Morley, Cullen got even more than he'd reckoned with.

'Adrian Morley had the ability to lead from within,' Cullen continued. 'He gave me the option to change the captaincy of the Warrington Wolves from Lee Briers to Adrian Morley, which was something that I didn't do lightly. In doing so it was very important to us as a club and to me as a coach that we didn't lose Lee Briers, but Adrian Morley's presence allowed me to do it.

'That also allowed Lee the freedom to express himself as a player and as a person without the pressure of captaincy and the management of the senior group.

'Adrian was an absolute dream to work with, both on and more importantly off the field. He constantly took us to another level. For example, I thought I'd done enough homework on him and knew him as a professional and personally. But in all honesty I completely underestimated the effect that he would have on the team, the club and even on myself.

'In his first training session he outpaced every three-quarter we had on the books during the sprint sessions. I knew he was quick, but I didn't know he was that quick!

When everybody was getting tired - and he was as well - he just ran faster and ran harder.

'At that time I had a certain structure that I wanted the team to play to, because when I arrived at the club they'd had so many coaches and different systems that the players were in a state of utter chaos. I brought in a system that meant they could manage themselves on the field and be accountable for their own performances. We provided a structure that allowed us to play in a very efficient way that used the talent we had, or didn't have, at that time.

'Yet when Adrian Morley breaks out of a scrum to take the second drive regardless of where the scrum was, I wasn't going to deny him that privilege. If we had a tap on the right-hand side of the field, and he wants to run past four of his own team-mates to carry the ball head first into the opposition's biggest player, I wasn't going to stop him doing it. He gave us weapons that we never thought we would have when I sat down with Simon Moran to discuss signing him.'

Cullen's opinion of Morley as a man reflects his admiration of him as a player.

'He was a complete and utter gentleman but I'd rather be his friend than fight him! The other players sat up and took notice of him, even though he is a man of few words. He led by example in the gym, on the training ground and on the field, and that was his approach to the game and to life. We bought an angel with a bit of a dirty face - he was no choirboy but he always aimed up. He could play out with the best of them, but never missed a step when it was time to work and deliver.

'At that point of the rebuild, we weren't at full salary cap, and we were limited with the budgets we had available to us to spend across 25 senior players. Adrian's contract is confidential and personal to himself and the club, but I was more than happy to shave down from having 25 senior players to roughly 21, with four Academy players brought up prematurely to accommodate Adrian. He didn't come cheap, but he was worth every penny Warrington ever spent on him times ten.'

So what of Morley himself? A self-confessed Bob Dylan fanatic, he was brought up a Catholic and still attends mass every weekend. While he was smashing opponents on the field, his former Warrington team-mate Matt King has recalled him dancing to 'Relight My Fire' at a Take That concert on one of the first times the pair met following the former Melbourne centre's move from Australia in 2008.

Rugby league has undoubtedly shaped Moz's life, however, so when asked about his own inspirational figures, it isn't surprising that he picks three fellow professionals.

'My first inspiration was my brother Chris - well both of my older brothers, Chris and Steve, to be honest,' Morley explains. 'But I say Chris in particular because he signed professionally with St Helens. He played in the same position as me, and him signing pro' gave me the drive to try and emulate him. I thought if he could do it, I could do it. He was always a good player, Chris, and I'd say that if he'd never made it. As it happens, he went on to play at Wembley and won Super League with Saints. But the fact that he signed professional was definitely inspirational and gave me a goal.

'He's three years older than me, and he was a bit of a rough arse of a player. He was never the most skilful, but he used to get stuck in. More often than not he'd be playing in a very poor Salford town team that would struggle against the other towns. But he always seemed to stick out, so I knew he had some talent. I remember him making the Lancashire side, and he was the only one from Salford that did. He could obviously play and went on to carve out a career for himself.'

Morley's next inspiration was a terrace hero from his days supporting Salford as a boy.

'When I was growing up I was - and still am - a Salford fan, and it was Harrison Hansen's dad Shane who was my hero there. His defence was awesome. He was quite unique in a lot of ways. There are obviously loads of overseas players here now, but there weren't many Kiwis here back then, and he had the old mullet with the long hair at the back, so he looked different from everybody else. He had a textbook tackling technique that was low and hard. He was club captain for a while as well and that's always impressive for a young lad.

'My favourite player of all time though was Ellery Hanley. He was just incredible. Although we were only on the field together for five minutes during my Leeds debut, at least I can say that I played with him. He doesn't need me to tell people how good he was. But growing up watching those great, star-studded Wigan sides, he stood out even then. Every time he played for Great Britain he did the badge proud, and he was rated incredibly highly by the Australians. I learnt that when I went over there.

'When I arrived in Australia they made a big thing about the other English players who had done well and Ellery was right up there. They probably rated Malcolm Reilly as number one, but Ellery was definitely number two. He won the Golden Boot as the best player in the world and rightly so. He was a magician really on the rugby league field, that's what drew me to him.'

This writer has his own Adrian Morley story to add. Starting out as a particularly young-looking reporter, approaching some of the sport's biggest names could be pretty daunting. But without exception, Adrian Morley would always return phone calls, go out of his way to come over and say hello at press conferences, and make an effort to ask how things were going. This continued for years, and was always put down to what everybody else said about the man - that you couldn't meet a more genuine bloke.

Which was absolutely true, of course, but there is more to the story.

Standing in as a touchline reporter for Premier Sports during the 2013 Rugby League World Cup, post-match the director wanted some additional reaction to the fearsome Italy versus Tonga clash that played out at the Shay. The floor manager that night, Chris Wood, had spotted Morley in the main stand, and having also dealt extensively with him through his own time at the RFL, asked the big man if he'd come over and say a few words. As always, Morley was completely forthcoming, although he admitted to having had a couple of beers with his mate during the match.

As he approached we shook hands and exchanged pleasantries, and while we were waiting to go on air, Morley turned to me and said: 'Tell Chris the story about how me and you first met.'

I had no idea. Literally no idea. I offered something along the lines of: '...it must have been an interview when you were first starting out at Leeds.'

Morley quickly responded: 'No, you know, at Wembley in 1996. I'd had a few drinks that day watching the Challenge Cup final and we had a right laugh in the crowd.'

The only problem was that I didn't go to the 1996 Challenge Cup final; I didn't make it to Wembley until 1999. It wasn't me.

But as recounted in his autobiography, Morley had certainly enjoyed his day down there to the full - he was almost arrested for running onto the field at the end of the game, trying to have a word with brother Chris, who had been left out of the side for the final. He burst out laughing. 'You must have an absolute double then. I could have sworn it was you that we were with that day. I bet you wondered why I always came over to ask how you were doing?'

Well I did after that! But in typical Morley style he made a big joke of the whole thing. And for the record, he has continued in exactly the same vein as he did before - always says hello, always asks how you are, always returns calls.

At the time of writing, Morley hadn't made a final decision on whether to continue playing in 2015, though his performances in the 2014 season for hometown Salford suggest there a few good miles in the old legs yet.

But whatever his future, the admiration for him so evident throughout the sport will continue for many years. And it is entirely reciprocal.

'When I first started playing the game I fell in love with it immediately,' he adds. 'I tried a number of other sports, but I knew straight away that this was the one for me. I've got a real passion for it - it provides you with so many skill-sets for life. It gives you discipline and camaraderie; it's the best team sport in the world as well as the toughest.

'You have to be tough just to play it, and that gives you good lessons in life. I feel blessed that I've had the chance to play rugby league as a job for so long, but if it wasn't my job then I'd still be playing for my local amateur side Eccles. It's an incredible sport, and I'm very proud of the fact that I've played it professionally. Hopefully, when I stop playing, I'll continue to be involved.'

● Gareth Walker is the editor of *Rugby League World* magazine and has been rugby league correspondent for the *Sunday People* since 2002. Covering the Championships for *League Express* allows him to keep in touch with the mighty Rochdale Hornets.

2. Man and Superman

Jamie Jones-Buchanan

I OFTEN have the privilege of talking to children, both in schools and community clubs, and try to impress upon them my belief that they all have something intrinsic and unique within; a virtue, an attribute, a physical ability - something that makes each of them special.

Finding out what that is, that's the real challenge.

All too often we want to model ourselves on someone else and while there's nothing wrong with being inspired or encouraged by others, the only way to fully be you, is by being you!

I recently went through the hardest 12 months of my professional life suffering a series of on-going injures, where

13 Inspirations

I regularly doubted my self-worth. Providentially, though, I came across an old Jewish poem:

> If I am I because I am I and
> you are you because you are you
> Then I am I, and you are you
> But
> If you are you 'because' I am I or
> I am I 'because' you are you
> then I'm not I and you're not you

If that's too heavy, then maybe Dr. Seuss does the trick:

> Today you are You, that is truer than true. There is no one
> alive who is Youer than You.

I realised that the only way to continue each morning was to be me, as well as I could be, but I've never met anyone who exemplifies that more than Matt King.

I first met Matt in 2011 while I was in an England training camp preparing for the Four Nations tournament.

We were told that, at the age of 17, he was paralysed from the neck down and is unable to breathe independently, following an accident in the first tackle of his first Academy game for the London Broncos back in 2004.

Matt's story is unrivalled and his challenges faced blow away any experiences I have had or anyone else I've met, particularly in the world of rugby league. He's an inspiring example of how to carry on, being everything you are each day, and with that outlook he's achieved some remarkable things. I was utterly captivated and in awe of what he told me while speaking to him for this chapter and so reproduce our conversation here in Matt's own words.

'I started playing rugby union when I was six for my local club, Biggleswade, and was there through the age groups.

'Matt Cook's dad saw me when we played against each other and asked me to come along to Bedford Tigers, his amateur rugby league team. I played both sports from about age 12 and was asked to go down to London Broncos to join their Scholarship programme when I was 14, and then on to the Academy.

'As a family, we loved sport. I played cricket and football for my school and county and was into scuba-diving - but rugby was my passion. I was never amazing, a decent club player, I think. League was something that just came into my life, I enjoyed playing it but didn't see it going anywhere long term; I just liked it for what it was.

'For my first academy match against Halifax in 2004, we traveled up in a minibus with all the tackle bags and arrived at The Shay the night before, sleeping on the floor in the bar - even though it was the big time, it wasn't all that glamourous. I don't know why but, looking back, I was so nervous about that game. It might have been instinct or my subconscious telling me that something was going to happen.

'We were due to play a curtain-raiser on the main pitch but it had rained very heavily and we were moved.

'When we did our warm-up, I remember dropping balls and making uncharacteristic errors, but I don't know if I am reading too much into this retrospectively. I was playing right centre; the match kicked off, there was the first hit up, second, third. I think their prop hit the ball in...

'I don't remember any pain, just remaining on the ground, trying to get up and not being able to.

'One of their players came across, leaned over me and said: "Are you alright, mate"? I tried to say something and couldn't speak. All I could do was mouth the word "help". They stopped the match.

'I'm not religious but a few things happened during that time to make me ask questions.

'There were only about 150 people watching the game, but the person who saved my life and resuscitated me had only done his training the day before. The fact that he was watching when I was hurt and it was his training that kept me alive until the paramedics arrived is too much of a coincidence.

'The paramedics and physiotherapists were asking if I could feel anything when they touched my toes. I couldn't. They asked if I could feel them touching my hand and again, no.

'I stopped breathing. I remember the paramedic leaning over me, holding my head, and asking him to let me die just thinking what my life would be like in a wheelchair.

'Having being active all my life until then and doing everything I wanted to, I can't express how frightening that thought was. I know it's a cliché when people say your life flashes before your eyes, but it did. I knew mine had changed forever.

'I was airlifted from the pitch to Leeds General infirmary and was unconscious for all of it. Because I had stopped breathing, they were unsure if I had sustained brain damage. But after two days they woke me up and my mum was there. They knew that if I recognised her voice there was a good chance that my brain was okay.

'I couldn't speak or move, all I could do was blink.

'Do you know who you are?' One blink.

'Do you know what your name is?' One blink.

'Do you know where you are?' One blink.

'Do you know what I am saying to you?' One blink.

'I knew that I had broken my neck and my life had changed forever. Everything I'd lived, loved and enjoyed but ultimately taken for granted was over.

'In hospital I was quite sheltered from the severity and was concentrating on trying to get better, but my family was affected just as much, if not more.

'They had to travel from Bedford, initially not knowing if I was okay. My mum is a nurse, so she knew the worst-case scenario.

'At that time there weren't any set procedures that came into play. These days you have the Rugby League Benevolent Fund and processes the RFL put in place to make sure that the player and family have a support network.

'Mum and dad were trying to do their best for me with minimal support. They had to do a lot of fundraising; it's because of them that I got out and am here today.

'I was drugged up and out of it. I didn't really understand all of what was happening and wasn't aware of the situation, but my family were.

'I spent nine months in hospital, which was terrible. My older brother had to come to terms with the trauma of what had happened to someone he grew up with, while my younger one, aged 12, lost not only his sibling for a year but his parents too, as their efforts were all centered on getting me home. There was so much for my family to take in.'

I HAVE learned, over the course of my playing career with Leeds Rhinos and England, that victory and defeat is almost a form of digital information; you win (1) or you lose (0).

The fact remains that, after either scenario, you have to wake up and carry on the next day.

Hollywood invariably tells us that, at the end of the film, everyone lives happily ever after. In reality, life is nothing like that. Everything in the physical universe is entropic, it degrades and wears away.

The real value comes with the love in the relationships you mold on the journey - something I have come to know as 'The Refiner's Fire'.

Winston Churchill said: 'Success is never final and defeat is never fatal, it is the courage to continue that counts.'

Waking up the next day and being all you can be, as well as you can be, is often as difficult after a win as it is a loss, but the only positive way is forward.

Jamie Peacock sent me this quote from Ernest Hemingway:

There is nothing noble in being superior to your fellow man, true nobility is being superior to your former self.

Or, for me, in a similar vein:

No one who puts a hand to the plough and looks back is fit for service in the Kingdom of God.   Luke 9:62

Matt was the person I remembered most as I came down the stairs carrying the base of the Challenge Cup at Wembley in 2014 after we'd beaten Castleford and buried our own rugby hoodoo.

Two years before, he carried the Olympic torch. He has continued on, using who he is, to help and inspire others.

He has a great mind that he went on to use as he studied law, as he again relates for himself:

'NINE months in a hospital is a long time to reflect. Everything I thought I would achieve in my life went completely out of the window. I had to re-evaluate my goals and what I wanted to do from then onwards.

'My parents practised tough love. They made it clear that I was a young boy with, hopefully, a long life ahead of me and I had to try make the best of it.

'It was clear that I was going back to school when I got out, to get my A-levels, go on to university, achieve my degree. Then, ideally, I would go on to build a career for myself, because it would have been no life if I had given up and sat at home watching Jeremy Kyle all day. I was always academic at school, worked hard, got good grades and in the long term that stood me in good stead.

'Before the accident I had contacted the RAF and was going through the initial application process. The lifestyle appealed to me, traveling the world flying planes and playing sport. But as a typical late teenager I was more interested in girls, friends and having a good time.

'My horizons were limited afterwards. It was either media, journalism or law. It had to be something you need your brain for, because that's all I have now.

'I studied history and geography when I went back to school then law at university and started work as a trainee solicitor in October 2011 in London.

'So far I've articled in personal injury, aviation and clinical negligence. I'm in my final year before I fully qualify as a solicitor and currently practising commercial litigation. My own experience, however, means I've got more to offer than just being a lawyer.

'Talking about that hopefully has a tiny impact on how others view their life. I definitely want to continue public speaking in the longer term.

'Rugby is a physical game. You can take the physical element out of it and play touch, but that isn't rugby. What happened to me was a freak accident. A team-mate came into the tackle to help and his knee hit me in the side of the head, which broke my neck.

'I don't hold any grudges, time is a healer.

'In hospital there was a lot of "Why me?", "Why do I deserve this?" But it became clear very early on that I couldn't continue thinking like that because it doesn't change a thing; it is what it is. I can't hold anyone else to account. If you play rugby, you accept the risks and you know what they are.

'You have to get on with your life, but there are still times when it hurts.

'I'm 27 now and my mates are beginning to settle down, have families and kids. You think these are a given and it was one of the first things that hit me in hospital, that they had been taken away from me.

'I do still have the dark days when I compare my life now to what it could have been, but I have to step out of that quickly. There are a lot of people worse off than I am.

'The 2012 Olympics created a massive buzz in the country and a feelgood factor. It was great to be a small part of that as a torch bearer and the legacy is living on.'

MATT does a lot of work for the NHS and I have been fortunate to hear him speak. His message is equally as pertinent in a sporting context as it is in a medical one.

The title of his talk is *Little Things Make A BIG*

Difference and two aspects of it stood out. On his display board he wrote these simple equations: $1 \times 1 = 1$, $2 \times 2 = 4$, $3 \times 3 = 9$, $4 \times 4 = 15$.

His audience instantly noticed the error, but that was exactly the point.

Too often we just see what is wrong, but he wanted the focus to be on the vast majority of what the NHS do that is right, especially given his direct experience.

He outlined how, on a difficult journey or in a team environment, those who emphasise the positive are the energy givers, as opposed to the ones who only see the number fifteen and are energy sappers.

As he notes, it is not a 'big thing' to change such a mindset and, when it comes to group relationships, it is not always what you do, but how, that ultimately makes the difference.

What I call the 'why' reason, struck home even more in the second point I embraced.

Matt talks a great deal about his family, friends and support network and particularly a nurse, Tracey, all of whom provided a loving care which, over the years, has helped empower him and kept him moving forward to achieve whatever he can with his life.

They provided his positive, not least by listening to his opinion of what was possible.

'IT was one split-second on the pitch, one dislocation which has changed my life forever. It is the most severe injury you can have without being brain-damaged, all because of an innocuous tackle 20 seconds into a match.

'It was the smallest thing that changed my life there

but, conversely, the smallest things also make the biggest difference to the success you can have in life.

'You can apply that in any walk of it, most people are able to do their job well but I find, with nursing in particular, it's not what they do - like giving an injection - it's how they do it, saying it with a smile and making you feel comfortable.

'Whether it's that one per cent extra when you are in training at rugby, or ten minutes more in the evening to make sure you get all your work done, those little elements make you stand out from the rest and allow you to overcome.

'In life, it is very easy to focus on what's not going well for you or the things that are wrong and forget all that is good. You need to interrogate the success and the things that work well because they make you the person you are.

'And there are always going to be things that you can improve upon or that aren't quite right.

'But just choosing to focus on what isn't perfect is destructive and was something that was applicable to me in hospital.

'The one thing that was wrong was my neck and the fact that my body wouldn't function anymore. But what I had was my mind, family and support network. They were what I had to focus on, because looking only at the one thing that wasn't right would get me nowhere.

'It's about focusing on your strengths and trying to overcome the obstacles or challenges.

'Certainly, the injury was one massive obstacle and it took a long time to get my head around it. But once I saw the light at the end of the tunnel and a path to recovery, going back to school, getting a job and enjoying my life again, it made not focusing on the one thing that is wrong so much easier.

'Fronting up instead of playing the victim is a terribly

hard choice but, once you make it, and commit to it, things are a lot easier.

'In the first few months afterwards there was a lot of seeing myself as a victim, rather than face up to the reality of what had happened and what my future life might look like compared to prior expectation.

'The turning point came one night when I spoke to one of the nurses who tried to tell me about ex-patients who had gone on to rebuild their lives successfully.

'Although, at the time, it was easier to discount what she said and not believe Tracey, it did plant a seed of hope. And that started me on my journey to actually becoming accountable for my future and, with the help of family and friends, rebuild it.

'There were instances along the way where I doubted myself.

'There was one occasion when I arrived at school and a group of students began laughing at me. I had to make a decision pretty much in that split-second, whether to give in and see myself as a victim again or confront what had just happened.

'Fortunately I took the harder option, but in the long run the better one.

'Everyone has in them a strength of character but you might need something to bring that out of you. For me it wasn't until I could see that glimmer of light at the end of the tunnel and it all became brighter.

'The closer I came to being discharged from hospital, the more I relied on the support of those around me.

'I wouldn't say there's anything different now that drives me, it's about getting up in the morning and just wanting to live your life the best you can be.

'My life changed in that split second on the pitch in

13 Inspirations

April 2004 - 04.04.04 - and my goals and aspirations altered along with it, but it didn't change the person I am or the fact that I want to make the most of this life.'

AS a professional rugby league player, I am a passionate believer in showing a willingness to give back, to pay for the unreturnable grace that was proffered to me on my journey as a sportsman; my gratitude knows no bounds.

Money is worth something, but time much more, particularly when used for the purpose of helping or inspiring others in a positive manner.

When I first met Matt King in 2011 he had come to Wembley before England's game against Australia.

Playing against the Kangaroos was the highest level I have ever performed at and, in retrospect, the toughest too.

Matt came to do the shirt presentation and he exceeded the occasion in the things he had to say and the message he portrayed.

Despite the challenges he faces, Matt is still actively inspiring and giving back in response to the love of others.

He is involved in charity events such as the New York Marathon and even paints pictures using his mouth for the rugby league benevolent charity. In recognition of his work, Matt was awarded an OBE.

He is a phenomenon.

'I RETURNED home from work one day and had a letter from the cabinet office. I guess it was a mixture of trepidation and excitement when I opened that envelope.

'The first paragraph said that the Prime Minister had nominated me for an award.

'I rang my mum straight away and I remember saying that if I could shake I would because it was genuinely something I never thought about, contemplated or wanted.

'I received the OBE in January 2012 from the Prince of Wales at Buckingham Palace. It was quite a surreal day, especially when you are surrounded by armed forces people who have done all these amazing feats in Iraq and Afghanistan.

'I felt a bit out of my depth, to be honest. But it's something I am proud of that will remain with me forever.

'I was incredibly fortunate in how the rugby league community rallied round, did fund-raising and in the support I received. Not just me but my family were too.

'If everyone else hadn't given up on me then it wouldn't have been fair to give up on myself.

'I remember a card I received from one little girl. She was three years old and it had a £1 coin taped inside of it; it was her pocket money to help the fund-raising and that was a gesture that really touched me.

'Chris Hawkins did a cycle ride from London to Perpignan to coincide with a Super League game. He was huge after I got hurt and in the years following.

'A charity called XIII Heroes raised a lot of money for injured rugby league players and we did the Great North Run together in 2006 and 2007.

'When I was in hospital, I would write with a mouth-stick and dabble with painting to help strengthen my neck muscles, but I was never particularly good. Once home, my grandma's friends liked doing paintings and she came round to teach me the basics and they sold a lot of Christmas cards from it for the benevolent fund.

'I applied to do the London Marathon and they said: "No!" So we thought the next best thing would be to go to America, where we did the New York version with the help of the Christopher Reeve Foundation.

'I had a great experience, again doing something I had thought not possible during my time in hospital.

'We are still in an on-going legal battle with the London Marathon organisers, about whether I can part. I've been declined the opportunity on a number of occasions in the past, based on the fact that my level of injury allegedly contravenes the rules governing the event, and/or on health and safety grounds.

'I am hoping to be on the start line in 2015. It would show that, even after a devastating injury, there's still a good life to be had.

'How many people are lying in hospital with a spinal injury thinking, what can I do? I know that if there had been somebody I could have looked towards who was doing things like that, it would have made a huge difference.

'While I am not looking to take unnecessary risks, you won't make the most of your life if you're not willing to stick your foot out there and dip your toe in the water of what is possible. Nowadays there are far too many people in places of authority who have forgotten why they're there.'

RUGBY league is an amazing game played by some astonishing people, no matter what.

You can be short and agile, tall and fast, wide and strong, meek or aggressive. It must be the most diverse sport in the world and if you have been in it for any length of time, you will have heard the phrase: 'Rugby league seems to attract the best kind of people.'

The sport so often reminds of the superhero narrative that society is fascinated with and which, to my mind, is just an amplification of what we see in ourselves.

Such outlandish figures, mythical legends and demi-gods have been in the human psyche for as far back as history records, and are just as massive in comic books and on the movie screen today.

The characters in them seem to have a diverse range of traits but fit within a virtuous framework.

They use their gift to serve others and while doing so wear a disguise to hide their true identity in humility.

A hero wants no recognition or exaltation for their acts as they work tirelessly and sacrificially, no matter what challenges are thrown at them.

Interestingly, I asked Matt if there was anyone outside of his relational sphere who inspired him or who he looked up to and the only person he could think of was Christopher Reeves, famous for playing the best-known superhero of them all ... Superman.

I can't do justice to Matt King in this chapter and fully illustrate his journey.

You will need to read his forthcoming autobiography to learn more about the man who, despite such a massively traumatic accident, made the decision to continue projecting the same love and support he had received from his family and close friends into the lives of so many others, while navigating himself above and beyond what he first thought possible.

From being the quickest to be discharged for that kind of injury in the hospital's history to the present day when he is preparing to get married and learn how to speak Polish, he has never stopped chewing up the challenges and inspiring those around him in the process.

For me, Matt King is a true superhero.

'I WAS incredibly fortunate, not just in hospital but also in the care I received right from the moment it happened on the pitch; the treatment that kept me alive and made sure my brain wasn't damaged through lack of oxygen.

'I have got so many people to thank along the line.

'Yes nine months in hospital is a long time - despite it being a record to the point of release - but to put it in context, other people are in hospital on a ventilator for two or three years.

'An aspect of that speedy recovery was that I was physically fit having played rugby at a fairly decent standard, which allowed me to combat the physical consequences of having a spinal cord injury. But it was all the jigsaw pieces in the support network that allowed me to get home from hospital. Looking back, I can reflect on the great care I had and if I am able to speak with NHS staff and nurses and doctors and give them a patient's perspective of the impact of both good and bad practice. I reckon that's invaluable because they can look to apply it for the benefit of others.

'I don't think by nature I am someone who likes confrontation, but I am a confident person and always have been. I know that if I want something, how to go about making sure it happens and I guess that determination helps too.

'This accident happened when I was young and was a situation that was forced upon me. I have had to get used to it, but I believe that how you get the most out of each day is what sets people apart.

'At first I couldn't imagine a future and, in the victim stage, thought no one would want to be with someone like me, but I met Ilona two years ago and we plan to get married next year.

'We recently went on a European road trip to Poland, which was fairly tough, 2,500 miles. I proposed in Prague on the way back, I had it all planned.

'It's beautiful in Prague and I had all these romantic locations in mind, but on the second day the rain came down and we went back to the hotel because we were drenched and I fell asleep. I woke up in the evening and thought I have to do it now, so I just did it there and then.

'I can't emphasise enough that time is a healer, it's been ten years now since the accident.

'Writing or talking about those times, having to reflect and get back inside the mind of a 17-year-old boy in his darkest days in hospital is tough, because it brings back memories that have been hidden away, suppressed and moved on from.

'It's like opening up old wounds, but in the intervening time I have come full circle and am now back leading a relatively normal life, whatever that is.

'I'm working, getting married, living independently and enjoying myself. I never thought all that was possible and now is the right time to write the full book of the journey.

'There's a fair bit going on in my legal and speaking careers and I'm trying to master a new language.

'I fancy Las Vegas for my stag do, but I might be getting a bit old for that now.

'My life is changing again.

'And I knew by how much the other day when Ilona recorded *Keeping Up with the Kardashians* and deleted the rugby league. I had to bite my tongue.'

● Jamie Jones-Buchanan signed for Leeds Rhinos as a 15-year-old and made his first team debut against Wakefield in 1999. Since when he has represented England in the second row and helped to win four Super League titles. He writes regularly for *Rugby League World* magazine.

3. Grapple, Tackles and Gunfire

Brian Heywood and David Gronow

RUGBY footballer, wrestler, war hero; as legends go, Douglas Clark was the genuine article. A Great Britain international forward either side of World War One, his was one of the greatest rugby league reputations of any era.

Born in Ellenborough on 2 May 1891, near Maryport on the Cumberland coast, his potential was evident as part of the Ellenborough national school team that finished runners-up to Aspatria in the County Schools. Upon leaving school he assisted in his father's coal merchant's business, a job in which he began to develop formidable strength. By the age of fourteen he could carry a hundredweight bag of coal under each arm, leaving seniors in awe at his enormous power.

Aged 15, Douglas joined local amateurs Brookland Rovers, playing in the intermediate (youths) under 18s. This coincided with a further move away from rugby union by the Northern Union, when Line-outs were abandoned and teams reduced from 15 to 13-a-side, creating more space on the pitch. He was also a natural Cumberland wrestler. Encouraged by winning his first championship at Braithwaite, he continued to wrestle throughout his rugby career and beyond.

Increasingly dominant in the Cumberland amateur game, he attracted the attention of professional clubs and signed for Huddersfield shortly before his 18th birthday in April 1909. He received a £15 signing-on fee and a further £15 on his first team debut. His father requested that he should find his feet in the reserve team for a time, but his giant stature ensured that he was soon top-grade material. He played his first match for Huddersfield at Hull KR on 25 September 1909, just five months after signing - much of that time being in the close-season. The following campaign saw him make his county debut with Cumberland, aged 19.

Douglas Clark went on to play 485 games in the claret and gold, still a Huddersfield appearance record, and gained 31 caps for Cumberland, a total bettered only by Joe Oliver.

Swiftly he became an important cog in Huddersfield's rapidly improving machine. Joining him in a formidable pack was Ben Gronow, signed from Bridgend RUFC shortly after kicking off the first Twickenham rugby union international, John Willie Higson, a key member of the famous Hunslet team that won all four cups in 1907-08, and the no-nonsense future Great Britain international Fred Longstaff from Halifax.

The centre-threequarters included mercurial Harold Wagstaff, probably the greatest and most creative player of the era, and the shrewd, aggressive Kiwi, Edgar Wrigley. Outside them were the devastating wingers local boy Stanley

Moorhouse and Australian Albert Rosenfeld. Bolstered by the arrivals of Aussie centre Tommy Gleeson and quicksilver half -back Johnny Rogers, Huddersfield began to accumulate a dazzling array of trophies. League Champions in 1912 and 1913, Challenge Cup winners in 1913, Yorkshire League winners in 1912, 1913 and 1914, and Yorkshire Cup winners in 1910, 1912 and 1914, they were the team to beat. It is a measure of their dominance that the 80 tries Rosenfeld scored in 1913-14 remains a record for the game in one season. What is more, it was made when the sport was much more low-scoring than it would become, and is unlikely to be beaten.

As well as a formidable scrummager and a ferocious tackler, Clark was very difficult to stop and Wigan could not cope in the 1913 Championship final when he charged over for a hat-trick of tries as Huddersfield won 29-2.

His international career spanned nine years from 1911 to 1920, and included the most famous international in rugby league history - the 'Rorke's Drift' Test at the Sydney Cricket Ground on 4 July 1914. Thrust against their wishes into three Test matches in seven days, it was a bruised Great Britain team, missing five first-choice players through injury, that took the field for the third. The use of substitutes was still half a century away and the tourists' problems were compounded when Douglas broke his thumb in the first half. Immediately after the interval he then dislocated his collar bone in a tackle. With Great Britain already depleted in numbers, he was strapped up and twice tried to continue before leaving the field in tears because he felt he had let his team-mates down.

Leading 9-3 at half-time, Great Britain were reduced to ten men early in the second half and at one point to just nine, while the hosts retained 13. Inspired by captain Harold Wagstaff, however, they held out for an extraordinary 14-6 victory. The Huddersfield captain was credited by the

Australian press with making up the missing numbers on his own. Wagstaff's speed of thought and movement in both attack and defence was never more evident.

The tourists returned on 26 September to a country at war. The players of Runcorn and Oldham responded to the call for volunteers en masse, but elsewhere the loss of players and supporters was gradual and the 1914-15 season was competitive. After an inconsistent start to the season, Huddersfield were galvanised by their returning internationals into a run of 36 wins and two draws from their last 38 matches. These included a 37-3 victory over St Helens in the Challenge Cup final and a 35-2 win over Leeds in the Championship final, Douglas scoring a try in the latter. Added to their Yorkshire League and Yorkshire Cup wins, these victories completed Huddersfield's 'Team of all Talents' four trophies cups in the season, emulating the achievement of Hunslet. The Swinton team of 1927-28 was the only other to achieve this.

By the end of the 1914-15 season the war had spread to many parts of the world, and was not going to be over any time soon. Nine of the Huddersfield team had signed up for the forces, crowds were dwindling across the game and the continued payment of players, already deemed by some to be immoral in wartime, was also financially unsustainable. From the summer of 1915 payments to players stopped.

Douglas continued to work as a self-employed coalman and, like the rest of the available players, to play for Huddersfield without remuneration. The players also took part in charity matches, some of which entailed Northern Union players rubbing shoulders with rugby union players for the first time since the rift of 1895.

The military did not recognise rugby's differences, and a handful of northern players who were in military training in rugby union areas played union in 1915-16. These included Gwynn Thomas, Wigan and future Huddersfield scrum-half who played for the Barbarians against South Africa in November 1915, and Huddersfield's Fred Longstaff, who played a match at Leicester in February 1916.

A charity match between a 'North of England Military Team' and an Anzacs military team at Headingley in April 1916 involved players from both codes on both sides. The North included Douglas Clark, Harold Wagstaff and Ben Gronow from Huddersfield, and the Leeds captain Willie Davies, while the Anzacs featured Huddersfield's Tommy Gleeson among others. Wagstaff had only seen one previous rugby union match and took the first half to find his feet, but ran half the length of the pitch to score what proved to be the match-winning try in the second. With Gronow kicking reliably, the Northern Union players scored a majority of the points in a 13-11 win. The North played two more charity matches, including a win over a Wales team at Anfield, all good practice for what lay in store for the Huddersfield stars.

Following conscription in the spring of 1916, Wagstaff, Gronow, Clark and Albert Rosenfeld were head-hunted by Major Stanley who was in charge of Army Service Corps Motor Transport Unit training at Grove Park, South London. He was also the Oxford University representative on the RFU and out to assemble the best rugby union team in the country.

Led by the inventive Harold Wagstaff, Huddersfield had revolutionised the Northern Union game, playing fast, open, attacking rugby in which even the forwards had license to improvise attacking play as temporary three-quarters when the opportunity arose. Wagstaff brought this approach into rugby union, which was still largely a game of static set-pieces, punctuated by kicking exchanges and occasional creative moves from the backs. It bewildered many opponents as the Army Service Corps won 25 of their 26 matches, scoring 1,110 points and conceding just 41. The RFU, though, was quick to nip any green shoots of reconciliation in the bud. On 4 October 1916, the RFU decreed that fraternisation with the enemy was purely a wartime measure.

The Army Service Corps school of 1916-17 was sent to war in April 1917. Wagstaff and Rosenfeld - named Rosen*field* on his army records to conceal his Jewish ancestry in case of capture - were posted to the Middle East, while Gronow and Clark were sent to the Western Front.

A non-commissioned officer with 352 Siege Battery Ammunition Column, Clark had a spectacular introduction there. Based at number 7 Siege Park on the Ypres Salient, he had a front row seat for a 17-day bombardment of the German lines. This was followed on 7 June by the detonation of 19 mines under German strongpoints along the nine-mile long ridge from the village of Wytschaete south eastwards to Messines. 450 tons of high explosives killed 10,000 Germans. The first entry in his diary from the front reads:

> I shall never forget Messines … the bombardment simply awful.

The attacks that followed were supported by the 168th Artillery Brigade, raised in Huddersfield at the start of the war and consistently one of the best brigades among the Allied forces. Their latest successes came at a price. On 13 June, Douglas Clark watched these 'Batteries from Huddersfield, each distressed, coming from Messines battle. I recognise about 200 … plenty of "Play up Huddersfield".'

Away from the immediate front line for much of the time, the motor transport units were thought to be on a 'soft number' by some of the infantry. The Army Service Corps rugby team had been harshly characterised as 'a dumping ground of professional slackers'. But as the use of spotter planes and observation balloons increased alongside the accuracy of longer-range artillery fire, the motor transport convoys were increasingly targeted, as Douglas was to find.

The MT, ASC*
B Haigh, Huddersfield, MT, ASC, 18 May 1917
(*who has been to over 200 breakdowns in two years in France*)

Some say we're not in danger -
The MT, ASC
But as a motor driver
I don't at all agree

Who takes the big guns up the line,
And ammunition, too;
And food for men and horses,
And brings back wounded, too?

Who has to travel awful roads
Which they have never seen
Without a light to lead them on,
And shell-holes in between?

Who helps our Tommy on his way
When weary and footsore,
And takes him to his 'little home',
Right to his dug-out door?

Who is it that goes up the line
To a place as hot as hell
For officers' cars and ambulances
That have been hit by shell?

13 Inspirations

Tis I, a first aid driver,
Have all this work to do,
And with wee Jock, my pal, to help
We've got them dozens through.

Let those who love to run us down
Just read these lines right through
And then I think without a doubt,
They'll give praise justly due.

* The Motor Transport, Army Service Corps

Douglas experienced the perils of the job for the first time on 12 June when he set out with a convoy of five lorries to deliver ammunition to the 156 Battery dump at Ploegstreet Wood, eight miles south of Ypres. On arrival they were cursed by an Officer 'for bringing lorries up in broad daylight ... We can easily see Fritz's observation balloons and watch events with a very wary eye.' The Battery Officer reluctantly allowed them to unload before dusk. They had just completed this when ...

… a German shell landed right on Dump, wounding Sgt of Battery in back. I would be 100 yards away on open road. Fritz shrapnel bursting all around ... find myself on ground knocked off footboards by drivers of lorry running to cover ... Fritz is trying to get it. We lay flat in a ditch, shrapnel bursting all over our heads past lorries. Battery want us to remove vehicle, but my drivers refuse. A bit of shrapnel hits door covering my legs. I run to lorry and try to take it to cover past our Battery, only to receive a curse from officer for drawing fire on them. I reverse it right back to Tree Avenue and Battery men give me a good cheer. Then officer thanks me. As soon as I get lorry under cover they stop shelling.

On 7 July the 352 Ammunition Column was moved, amid 'nasty rumours concerning our new position', to a Siege Park on the southern outskirts of Ypres. Thereafter they were frequently delayed by congested roads and increasingly targeted with gas shells, a narrow escape on 16 July precipitating regular gas drills but these did not help Douglas on 24 July.

> We are about to unload. Fritz sends over shrapnel. Gets in Dump which spreads all over lorries and, of course, we get it. He kills one man and two lose their arms. I am very weepy.
>
> We help bandage poor fellow up. He sends over his beastly Chlorine gas. We put them in lorry. Driver missing. I take helmet off to call for driver, but have to put it on again. Driver turns up and takes wheel, nearly ditches us. I take off my helmet to drive, manage to get to hospital. Find two of wounded dead. I collapse and taken to gas hospital. Eyes, chest, throat very bad. Sick, sick.

On 27 July Douglas was still being treated for gas poisoning when …

> … hostile aircraft drop gas bombs near Park. Wear helmet for one hour. Bombardment sounds like some monster giant wheel crushing everything in its wake. Everybody confident of coming battle.

The coming battle, scheduled for 31 July, was the Battle of Pilkern, the first phase of the Battle of Passchendaele.

Douglas's diary records regular sporting fun at the siege parks of the ASC, where he wrestled and enjoyed games of chess, cricket and football - at least until 27 October when a bombardment destroyed their goalposts. On 16 October he delivered a talk to his comrades about the 1914 British Northern Union tour of Australia. As well as maintaining morale and fitness, battalion sports often involved target practice. As Laurie Magnus commented in *The West Riding Territorials in the Great War*, with: '...play imitating work ... The old saying about the playing-fields of Eton and the battle of Waterloo recurs to memory ... The preparation for war in sport was illustrated again and again.'

Douglas Clark witnessed preparations for Passchendaele on 30 July when, still recovering from chlorine gas inhalation, he returned to hospital at Poperinghe.

> ... eyes not quite as well today ... RAMC men prepare for 50,000 wounded, marquees all along road ... bombardment to commence after midnight. After dusk, roads full of limbless and Red Cross. 12pm [midnight] Mr Preedy and myself take up our position to watch bombardment from top of lorries ...
>
> ... at 3.50am witness the sight of our lives. 3 mines go off and guns open in full. Such a bombardment the like of which this war has never seen. Then the line just looks white hot and Fritz is soon in trouble sending SOS Green and Red star shells up along the front.
>
> I have never seen fireworks half so beautiful ...
>
> ... We all wonder if it's possible for a human being to live in it ... but the left flank of enemy holds fast. We bombard this flank all day ... our men advance ... but owing to such bad state of no-man's land, we cannot take guns up to support ... We bombard all night, but rain sets in. Conditions awful, out of question going over.

The mud for which Passchendaele is notorious was increasing by the hour. On 1 August, Douglas wrote: 'It never stops raining ... ground awful', and on 2 August, 'Rains all day. Cook house blown down.' There would be only brief respites from the rain over the next four months. The Allies pounded the 13-mile battle front with 4.25 million shells until mid-August, but amongst their successes they destroyed the many dykes and ditches that drained the low-lying, clay-based terrain. It created the worst underfoot conditions for an attacking force in the history of the British Army.

Tanks were negated, fire and movement - any sort of movement - was problematic, and the deepest German lines were six miles away. The water table was so high that there were few German trenches. Instead, the land was defended by dozens of pillbox machine gun posts with overlapping fields of fire. Relatively stationary behind these outposts and their deeply wired first, second and third Hindenburg Line defences, the Germans' quickly disrupted attempts by the Allies to coordinate battalions, tanks and artillery in the same attack.

On 16 August Douglas Clark received a widely circulated extract from a 'Zurich telegram.'

We must hold our positions between the seas and our lines or we shall lose the war entirely. The fate of Germany is now being decided in Flanders.

On 22 August he was part of a munitions convoy that delivered 800 rounds of ammunition to three different batteries. At 352 Battery's position ...

... get guns unlinked and into position, then we start unloading shell ... when Fritz sent over a shrapnel shell which burst over my head. I gave myself up as a goner, about 15 pieces hit my steel helmet and my back. I thought of home, but luck was with me and my helmet.

Shrapnel fairly splintered off it and nearly choked me with smoke. Cox was 10 yards from me and gave me up as lost. Pleased to report only damage, a cut on little finger, so I carry on ...

On a foggy 30 September, Douglas Clark delivered ammunition to the front line along the Menin Road.

Fritz is knocking hell out of [it]. 4 motors destroyed, and man's greatest friend the horse, poor beasts, are lying dead or dying on this road this morning ... would turn anyone. We arrive at Battery just as bombardment of ours start. It's hellish awful, poor Bosch ... Guns everywhere you look blending fire. This is a real war, a wonderful, splendid, inspiring, awful sight I shall not forget.

By 26 October the Allies were within 500 yards of Passchendaele. That afternoon Douglas Clark and the 352 Siege Battery Ammunition Column made several deliveries, the last of them to the 352 Siege Battery almost a mile beyond Prazinburk Ridge, near St Jean. As Douglas recorded, their orders were taking them ever-closer to the front line.

Death on every side. 12 tanks destroyed ... count 20 horses and 8 men dead. Wounded coming in. Splinters from Fritz shell hit my legs. Flying everywhere ... Pours with rain and up to knees in slush, no words could explain condition, still we all see what Salient looks like. We return to Park ... have supper and turn in wet through.

Three days later they were again unloading at 352 Siege Battery's dump when ...

... Fritz starts shelling, simply hellish. We have to unload ourselves as men have taken cover, horses and men flying for their lives. Grenadier Guards … are detailed to unload us. After one lorry they scoot and we never see them again. I have never seen anything so awful as this before, death at every side.

Then a shell struck part of the dump where the Guards' captain and some of his men were sheltering. Douglas tried to organise a rescue, but …

> … Three officers and lots of men refuse to help me, they run like March Hares.

Entering alone, he found them 'badly wounded from some burning cartridges,' and helped them to the relative safety of his lorry, before continuing his journey of deliveries.

> … officer comes up and thanks me, says I'm a brick. I breathe a silent prayer for four hours and think every minute my last. Words fail to express this scene, blood everywhere you look, dead men and wounded. Those fine stretcher bearers.

The pack mule drivers of the Royal Field Artillery unloaded on Prazinburk Ridge, as it was 'not fit to take horses further' yet Douglas and his colleagues delivered to 352 Siege Battery a mile further along the same road. There, the Battery men refused to leave cover to help as the lorries were unloaded.

> There's not a soul in sight excepting men trying to find a better hole … You can see shell explode long before you hear the noise of shell travelling through air and explosion.

A shell erupted close to their position and burning fragments set fire to some of their shipment of cartridges. He and his co-driver fled, fearing a major explosion, but returned when their wounded passengers could not make their escape. Extinguishing the blaze, they returned to their Siege Park.

> The awfullest day in my life so far. My lucky star.

For how long could Douglas's luck hold? Their next delivery was to the same area in the early evening two days later. They drove over Prazinburk Ridge, keeping 200 yards between each lorry. As an extra precaution, they planned to wait until each lorry had not just unloaded but returned before starting out on the last 200 yards.

> It is now quite dark and wind favourable for Fritz gas. All guns his side of Bavaria House in action … Mr Preedy and I rode on first vehicle. We had not gone very far until we found the gas very bad … so we pulled up to warn drivers, Mr Preedy going back to following lorries. I took ours forward to unload … the place was deserted, so first and second driver and myself started unloading. I pulled off my helmet 3 times, doing so I was almost overcome. At this point one of Fritz's green lights flared up, and then the place was turned into hell. I doubt if ever Fritz has sent over so many shells on such a small stretch as he did round us, even putting the shelling of the previous days in the shade. I received a nasty wound in the left arm and I thought it certain all would be killed. I ordered boys to go back and take cover near the other lorries. Here I found Mr Preedy and reported I was wounded. He wanted to take me to hospital, but I refused to leave lorries. Shells were falling in front, behind and on all sides … we decided to get lorries out of this …

With some difficulty, Douglas turned his lorry round. Then …

> … a shell burst, hitting me in the abdomen and chest and throwing me some distance.

The blast threw him over a hedge into a pool of water.

> I was bleeding very heavy from stomach and having lost my gas helmet, thought the end must be near. It's then a man starts to think of the dear ones at home and I prayed I might just be able to see them to say 'goodbye', when another shell threw me back onto the road …

As the men emerged from cover they found Douglas 'lying on the road with almost all of his clothing torn off by the force of the explosions.'

> … I was picked up and taken to Ypres Dressing Station (the Prison) and my wounds dressed. The journey left me very weak from loss of blood, it was simply murder.

From there he was moved to Number 10 Casualty Clearing Station outside Poperinghe. Doctors found a total of eighteen pieces of shrapnel embedded in his left arm, abdomen and chest, one piece penetrating 'perilously near his heart.' His only chance was an immediate operation.

Passchendaele Ridge and village were captured by the Canadian 1st Division, supported by devastating fire from the Huddersfield men in the 168th Artillery Brigade, on 6 November. Casualties numbered 260,000 Germans and 310,000 Allies. Among these was Douglas Clark, who was fighting for his life.

He came round from the operation to remove shrapnel from his chest and abdomen at 4am on 1 November, about eight hours after receiving his injuries. He endured a 'very bad' 48 hours, but it is testimony to the skilful surgery and to his sportsman's strength, endurance and determination that he gradually recovered. On 9 November he was transported to base hospital at Boulogne, where the ward was 'a large marquee with 32 beds and very comfy considering wild elements.' Three days later he was marked 'for blighty.' He sailed from Boulogne to Dover and by 17 November was in the Northern General Hospital, Lincoln.

On 27 November his parents arrived from Ellenborough just as he learned that his courage had earned him the Military Medal. He was transferred to Huddersfield's Royds Hall War Hospital on 17 January 1918, and to convalesce at Honley District War Hospital ten days later.

Invalided out of the war with 95 per cent injuries, Douglas was told that he would jeopardise his life if he returned to his rugby and wrestling careers. Defying medical expectations, he rejoined his Motor Transport Unit on the Western Front. In 1919, he resumed his position in the Huddersfield pack, helping the club to win the Yorkshire League, Yorkshire Cup and Challenge Cup. The Team of all Talents were on course for four cups again, but the Championship final against Hull was played with the Great Britain tourists already sailing for Australia. Aboard were Huddersfield's Harold Wagstaff, Johnny Rogers, Gwynn Thomas, Ben Gronow and Douglas Clark. In their absence, a late Billy Batten try deprived the Fartowners of their fourth trophy of the season.

Douglas's highlight of the tour down under came against New Zealand at Wellington. Great Britain had reduced a 10-0 deficit to 10-6 when he powered over for a try, Gronow's conversion sneaking an 11-10 win.

Douglas played for Huddersfield until 1929, retiring

at the age of 38 as part of another Championship-winning team. Fittingly, there was a memorable encore. In December 1929 he was called out of retirement and captained Cumberland to an improbable 8-5 win over the Australians.

Douglas's retirement from rugby league coincided with the formal organisation of professional wrestling in Britain. In 1930 Sir Atholl Oakley organised the first all-in wrestling tournament at the Lanes Club in Baker Street, London. Douglas beat Oakley in the final to become the first British all-in wresting heavyweight champion.

Amidst an upsurge in interest, he topped the bill at wrestling halls for the next eight years. He beat the best around, including Jackie Pye, Bill 'Bulldog' Garnon and the USA champion Jack Irslinger, twice becoming the heavyweight all-in wrestling world champion. Reputedly 'the strongest man on the planet', he toured Australia in 1934 and 1936, and remained the man to beat until he was emphatically beaten in a much anticipated bout against the great American Jack Sherry in 1938. By then Douglas was 47 years old. He eventually retired from the ring in 1941 at the age of 50.

Throughout his sporting glories, Douglas ran to keep fit and continued to work as a coalman. The site of him carrying a hundredweight sack of coal under each arm was a comforting feature of Huddersfield. In middle age he offered wise counsel on the Fartown committee and was a keen golfer at the Outlane and Huddersfield clubs. He often returned to his boyhood haunts on the Solway coast where he enjoyed fishing, swimming in the sea and running for miles on the sands.

Then, in January 1951, Douglas contracted influenza. To the shock of all, he never recovered and died at his home in Birkby on 1 February. He was 59. Douglas always thought of Maryport as his home town, and, at his request, he was buried in the Maryport cemetery.

In 1999, Douglas Clark was among the first inductees to the Huddersfield Hall of Fame, and in 2005 he joined his Fartown team-mates Harold Wagstaff and Albert Rosenfeld as one of 17 inductees to the Rugby League Hall of Fame.

A letter survives that he wrote to the Huddersfield players, probably from one of his wrestling tours of Australia. In it, Douglas reveals his philosophy, developed from a lifetime's experiences in sport, and war.

> It is excellent
> > To have a giant's strength;
> But it is tyrannous
> > To use it like a giant.

● David Gronow, who sadly died shortly after this chapter was written, was the official historian of Huddersfield Giants RLFC and grandson of Ben Gronow who, along with Douglas Clark, was at the heart of the pack in Huddersfield's legendary 'Team of all Talents.'

● Brian Heywood is manager of the *Huddersfield Rugby League: A Lasting Legacy* heritage project. An ex-teacher and writer of sports history articles and books, he owns the Sports Inspire Educational Publishing company.

13

4. True Colours

Tony Hannan

'IN the far-off times of my South Leeds childhood, in our back-to-back two-up-one-down, my parents and I looked forward keenly to a weekly incident. Every Saturday morning a tall black youth strode jauntily along our cobbled street. Black men were so scarce in Hunslet that we rushed to the window, twitched the net-curtain, and watched the young man go past. The same thing happened, I am sure, at every window along that street.'

Those are the words of the late renowned playwright Willis Hall, in his afterword to one of the most enthralling rugby league autobiographies ever published. The book is *Born On The Wrong Side*. Its author: Theodore Cecil Thompson.

13 Inspirations

To turn its pages is to meet a man for whom setbacks - and what setbacks - were mere sparks of opportunity. Cec as he was known to his friends, i.e. anyone with whom he came into contact, tended towards a, shall we say, positive disposition. A classic self-starter despite an impoverished background that was less sport more misery memoir, he fought his way to the pinnacle of a game that he had only played three times before signing for Hunslet in 1948 for what would back then have been the enormous sum of £250.

As Hall goes on to add, what the myrtle and flame got for their money was: '…dogged and unbridled enthusiasm'. And it would be those very same qualities that, off the field, drove an even more impressive rise.

It is problematic to define anyone chiefly by reason of colour but, in Cec Thompson's case, how can one not? Canny businessman, economics lecturer, international rugby league player, journalist, author and more he may well have become, but as the very title and opening line of his own story make abundantly clear, from the most unpromising of beginnings the issue of race was ever-present.

And race in both senses. Thompson's days with us - he died, aged 85, in 2011 - were spent at full pelt, a fact to which the chapter headings also attest. 'Walking' … 'Running' … 'Learning' … 'Teaching' … and then at last, 'Reflecting'. 'Doing' words the lot of them, as the future comprehensive and grammar school master would no doubt have taught.

'I didn't know I was a "nigger" until I was twelve,' *Born On The Wrong Side* begins, with a trademark matter-of-factness that still carries the power to shock, and we're off on a 250-page dash that is as exhilarating as it is extraordinary.

Cec Thompson was born in County Durham in 1926 to Florence Greenwell, a miner's daughter, and William Alfred Thompson of Port of Spain, Trinidad, who died aged

39, just months before his son's birth. Though Cec therefore never knew his father, a painter and decorator by trade who he supposes took his name from '...some British plantation owner who had imposed his patronym on the slaves in his possession', oldest brother Robert remembers William as: '.. a tall handsome man who attracted people's attention the moment he walked into a room.' It seems fair to assume that this must have been down to the colour of his skin, although remaining photographs equally portray him as a proud and '...impeccably groomed black Edwardian in a wing collar, with a gold watch and chain adorning his waistcoat and a handkerchief in his top pocket.'

Florence was white, having met William when he arrived in England's north-east as a corporal in the West Indies Regiment during World War One. With the war over, he stayed and the pair began a family, moving to Yorkshire when their father won a contract to append gold leaf to the walls of Leeds Town Hall. It was in that city that Cec was conceived and it was there that William died, the result, writes Thompson, of sand in the spleen from time spent serving in Egypt. He is buried in Armley cemetery.

Such a pairing was, to use Cec's own phrase: 'an unusual alliance for that time.' Perhaps, he wryly concludes, being a miner's daughter, '...she was used to black faces.' But in any case, leaving aside racial implications, the death of the major breadwinner upon a clan that by Cec's arrival included four children under seven (Robert, another brother Aubrey and sister Linda the others) was bound to have a dire impact.

And so it did. Destitution swiftly followed as 26-year-old Florence, pregnant with Cec, struggled to get by. The house that came with William's job was reclaimed, along with Linda's pram when payments could not be met. So Florence took her brood back to Durham, where Cec entered the world, and then returned to Leeds where an organisation called the Waifs and Strays Society entered the picture. A grateful Thompson would ever after lend it financial support, even with scarcely a penny to his name. 'I shall never forget how they helped my mother and all the benefits I received from my fostering and orphanage upbringing,' he writes of a turn of events that saw his siblings dispersed far and wide - Bob to Merseyside, Aubrey to Kent, baby Cec to a widow in Warminster and Linda, eventually, to St Chad's orphanage in Headingley. He was not someone given to self-pity.

Thus began a childhood that after that spell of sterile and perfunctory foster parenting in Wiltshire, saw five-year-old Thompson himself packed off to an orphanage in Weston-Super-Mare. From there, it was up to Tattenhall, Cheshire, where on a float in the village carnival he took the part of an Indian prince. Thompson remembers much of this time as having been secure, cheerful enough and clean, though he seems to have been a solitary child who found it difficult to mix. He was, he says: '...well on the way to becoming the ponderous, slow-thinking, pretty hopeless good-for-nothing which characterised the first twenty years of my life.' That ante was upped by a move to a third and final orphanage in Tynemouth, where bullying was added to the timid young fellow's problems:

> They used to form a circle round me and push me round and round, making me ricochet faster and faster until I was hurtling round the encircling bodies. My shirt would always get torn as I was grabbed and then hurled away, the gang hilarious from seeing this wretched coon becoming increasingly dizzy and woebegone.

And, of course, any boy with a torn garment was caned.

It was a miserable spell when beatings were the norm and resentment at the unfairness of it all began to seethe and fester within, lightened only by a day-trip to see his maternal grandparents, themselves enduring grinding poverty locally but noble and loving nonetheless. They gave him his first experience of hugs, kisses and other such open displays of affection, reducing him to tears: '…I was getting my first taste of family life,' he said of that single solitary visit.

Until, in 1938, the mother with whom he never quite managed to bond married Edwin, a baker from Leeds, and one by one the Thompson children gravitated to Meanwood. The happy ending though would have to wait. Soon, World War Two intervened - with Bob serving in Burma, Aubrey in the RAF and Cec eventually sailing off to Singapore with the Royal Navy. Before then, however, an emotionally-repressed youngster had his first blatant encounters with bigotry.

Made to feel an outcast by pointed fingers and racist insults - 'Did you come out of your mother's arse?' - and lacking in formal education, Cec's sense of rootlessness took over. He began to wet the bed and develop feelings of inadequacy. 'Was there nowhere to hide?' he writes. 'The only place in which I felt safe was the cinema - we were all the same colour in the dark. But the lights always came back on.'

Aside from a spell evacuated to Doncaster on the outbreak of war, much of the rest of Thompson school-aged years were spent - we might more accurately say served - at Sheepscar, where 'future criminals did their training' and 'the heroes were the gangleaders and pimps, characters out of *Brighton Rock*.' Here at least, shyness came in handy. Avoiding the '…seedy style of life they aspired to, stealing, gambling, boozing, fast cars, fast chicks and the unsteady flit from pub to pub, prison to prison…', he hung on until leaving aged 14 and then went down one blind alley employment-wise to another. Most often that was as a labourer - 'I was just a beast of burden really, a clod hopper' - but one job at least, feeding a metal furnace at Kirkstall Forge on sweaty shifts eight hours long turned him, he says, into:

> ...a kind of colossus. My body strength enabled me to perform spells of manual labour that were almost superhuman. I became a youth of truly enormous strength and power. Little did I realise that I was also being prepared for my rugby career in the years ahead.

THAT particular turn in Cec Thompson's fortunes came in 1947, upon leaving the Navy he had joined three years earlier.

Far from broadening minds, encountering people who Rudyard Kipling had called 'lesser breeds without the law' in places like Colombo and Mumbai (then Bombay) had shown Cec superiority towards other races was indoctrinated in his countrymen: 'The British servicemen referred to these natives as "wogs", and I was a wog too in their eyes.' Nor was he in much of a position to challenge their prejudices:

> With my lack of formal education, social graces and self-assurance, I could do little to prove that non-whites were equal in the sight of God. Indeed, my naval adventure ... reinforced and perpetuated my chronic inferiority complex. I returned to civilian life wallowing in self-doubt.

Help, though, lay just around the corner. At Yorkshire Copper Works in Hunslet to be precise, where Thompson almost immediately found employment as a lorry driver's mate.

The driver in question was a rogue named Harry who flattered young Cec to the extent that he ended up doing all the work, lugging eight loads of coke a day from railway goods yard to factory. But still, it continued to build strength and stamina. So when, in 1948, this by now six-foot 14-stone rugby novice was press-ganged into representing the firm in a works tournament in nearby Bramley, he proved to be a more than useful acquisition.

Interestingly, as with Ikram Butt from Leeds's Muslim community much later and other league players of ethnically diverse backgrounds, Cec forever denied possession of any skill or ability, attributing his achievements to physical build and, most crucially, boundless enthusiasm. Whether that was simply the truth or typical humility, his display that day impressed the scouts of Hunslet, Dewsbury and Bramley.

The first of those seemed particularly keen: 'Where doz tha' git all tha' bloody energy fra'? Tha laiks a reet gud game,' asked their representative. So keen in fact that the club almost immediately snapped up this rawest of recruits - 'I felt like a millionaire' - and he went straight into an 'A' team reserve match versus Castleford.

A quite different Harry from that era, current Leeds Rhinos president Harry Jepson OBE, in situ at Headingley since the early 1980s, but before then a widely influential figure at then major contenders Hunslet, puts a name to the scout that spotted an athlete who subsequently described his ascendancy into professional sport as being: '...like entering a dream-world as exhilarating as falling in love.'

'Cec was recommended to Hunslet by committeeman Albert Howarth who had seen him play for the Copperworks at Bramley and brought him to the club,' says Harry, 94, but with a sparkle in his eye for rugby league that has dimmed not one jot with the passing of the years. 'When I first saw him what impressed me most was his tackling. I remember his early games well. Off the field, he was virtually illiterate.

13 Inspirations

'On journeys to away games, Les Williams, a teacher, and Jack Evans, a civil servant, used to sit with Cec and the *Reader's Digest* doing 20 words - learning what they meant and how to pronounce them - it was a feature of our coach trips. He wasn't really a teller of tales, more a listener. The sport took him to places he could never have contemplated.'

The most immediate place it took him was Hunslet's first-team second row, where Cec made ten appearances before fracturing the tibia in his left leg, forcing him to sit out several months of his debut season. Reality had intervened.

> When I was promoted to the first team, I could hardly cope with my excitement and the highly charged atmosphere of the game. The speed and skill of the players left little time for thought. Most of the action is instinctive, a split-second's hesitation earns a tackle like a sledgehammer's blow. I soon realised that at first-team level the physical punishment ... is ferociously demanding; and total commitment was needed simply to keep one's place.

In fact, not only did Cec keep his place, but 'Darkie' Thompson, as the press and rugby league in general took to calling him, went on to excel to the extent that in 1951 he became the very first black Englishman to represent Great Britain, following in the pioneering 1947 footsteps of Welshman Roy Francis (Barrow) and brothers Jimmy and Val Cumberbatch (Broughton Rangers and Barrow), who played for England in the 1930s.

The journey to that point, though, had not been easy. One of the most brutal winters Britain had ever seen was not a good time to be hobbling about on crutches, and to cap it all his mother Florence died of cancer, leaving her youngest son once again feeling abandoned and alone. Close to giving up on rugby league before he had really begun, he headed south to find work in London before being forced to hitchhike home after being forced to sleep 'exhausted, unwashed and hungry' on a Hyde Park bench.

Once back in Leeds, he again picked himself up and became a member of the Hunslet 'A' team that won the 1949-50 Yorkshire Cup, once more making occasional appearances in the first team. And it was a period during which he began to wise up, not only to the win-at-all-costs mentality of professional rugby league, but even among team-mates who had at least one eye on their own self-interest:

> Once I was supporting my second-row partner, who had made a break with only one man to beat for the try-line some ten metres away. I called for the ball; he looked at me but ran on to try to beat his one remaining opponent but was tackled in possession. After the match, I realised he was playing for his place in the team and in that context he saw me as a rival.

Mainly, though, he was welcomed into the Hunslet throng in an area south of the city felt to be 'rough', in comparison with 'posh' Headingley to the north. For institutionalised Cec, the experience seems to have been a major eye-opener. A self-confessed pacifist, he didn't swear, smoke or, at that stage in his life, consume alcohol. He also had a fear of women which, along with having a name like Cecil, led many in 'a tough bunch' thinking he must be gay: '…which is not a reputation anyone would want in professional rugby,' he writes, years before Gareth Thomas turned that particular expectation on its head. His colour wasn't the only thing that marked him out as different.

Nevertheless, the Hunslet players, he tells us in *Born*

On The Wrong Side, are men he will be indebted to for the rest of his days:

> They were hard but courageous and generous too. Because they knew I always gave my best on the field, they looked after me. A player can be easily hurt if the opposition is playing flat out and there is a collision between an opponent's fist and your face, but my team-mates always protected me from unfair play. In fact, I think the opposition eventually learned to leave me alone, knowing that twelve of my mates would retaliate if I went down. It gave me a hugely comforting feeling.

The home fans too took to this unlikely hero in their midst. They asked for autographs that Cec, to his embarrassment, struggled to sign. This, though, simply prompted him to improve his handwriting and, while he was at it, learn how to make casual conversation. The contrast in lifestyles of the club directors and that of players and fans ignited a growing social conscience, and soon he was given a standing ovation by a crowd of 9,000 after having helped Hunslet to see off Castleford at Wheldon Road, 17-8.

'Rugby league is still seen by many people in this country as a bit of a North of England eccentricity,' he wrote in 2004, 'a sort of rugby union game adapted to the primitive needs of northern peasants. It was bad enough to be black. Now I found, if I told anyone I played rugby league, that I had acquired yet another label.' He went on: 'How much lower down the social scale could one go than be seen as a black, uneducated, rugby league player who was also an unskilled manual labourer?' In an outcast sport, Cec Thompson at last felt he belonged.

Thanks to the arrival of television and promotional

efforts of BBC commentator Eddie Waring, rugby league in the 1950s was, however, starting to make greater in-roads into the national consciousness. And it was Waring who, via his column in the *Sunday Pictorial* newspaper, began to publicise Thompson's exuberance far and wide.

By 1951, with a first-team place at Hunslet cemented and local hero status assured, Great Britain did indeed come calling, just four years after he'd first trotted out nervously onto the pitch with Yorkshire Copperworks. Cec was picked for October's first Test with New Zealand, won 24-15 at Bradford's Odsal Stadium. During the build-up, Waring famously wrote that if Thompson had not been chosen '…the selectors must be racists.' Cec himself noted that: '…there must have been plenty of Hunslet supporters in the crowd because I got a great ovation…' before admitting that he had played well. Though not, he is quick to posit, to the extent of Alfred Drewry's thrilled report in the *Yorkshire Post*:

> It's queer how blind people can be to facts. I had only seen Thompson once before the Test, and was struck by the natural way he seemed to fit in with rugby league style. "Oh, he's all right," said a very good judge of Yorkshire players, "but he isn't top class."
>
> Now if there was a forward on the Great Britain side who looked top class in the Test where Thompson came to judgement, it was the Hunslet living bronze. His poise, his grace, his swerve, and lithe easy action were a delight to see. He reminded me for all the world of those old bronze figures that were once all the go for mantel decoration. An athlete poised with one foot on a ball, needing only wings to be too good for this earth.'

The *Daily Herald*, meanwhile, headlined the match: Hunslet's

'Darkie' One of Britain's Heroes', and went on to praise his 'deep thrusts'. In any event, Cec was selected for the televised second Test in Swinton also, two games entitling him to an international cap, a real ding-dong affair won by the hosts 20-19 after the Kiwis had looked like springing a surprise.

With the series won, other players were given a run and Cec's brief Great Britain career came to an end, though he did continue to make county appearances for Yorkshire and, the following year, represented an Empire XIII against a Wales XIII won 29-16 by the former, in Llanelli. He also narrowly missed selection to the 1958 Lions Tour down under and went to France, first with England and then on tour with Hunslet, further stirring the imagination of an insecure lad who had to contend with teasing and stares in every new environment he entered. By common consent, in a less prolific time for back-row forwards, many more caps would have come his way.

Yet with his profile at its peak and the world at his feet, Cec's weekly walks down Willis Hall's cobbled street were moving to a conclusion. One more season followed in 1952-53 - his last game in an overall 96 for the South Leeds side being a 21-5 away defeat to Halifax. And then he was off, up to the far North West coast, on a still more impressive eight-season adventure at Workington Town before, finally, bringing the curtain down as coach at injury-hit Barrow, with a two-game swansong against Bramley and Blackpool in season 1961-62.

The impetus behind that move - for which his market value had now risen from £250 to £2,500 - was marriage to his very first girlfriend Barbara, to whom he had been engaged after just eighteen months. The communal reaction to this mixed couple made him appreciate his parents' experience and left him feeling like '…a fox being chased in the countryside by hounds. I imagined I had to be wily to survive.' Nor was living with the in-laws particularly helpful and the already arguing couple decided that a change of scenery would do them good.

And so it did for a while; nothing could now knock Cec off his stride it seemed. He fell in love with the Lake District. He was financially stable. He rubbed shoulders with middle class people, got invited to their dos. Town being a cosmopolitan club with ambition, he met Australians whose liveliness and self-assurance he found 'illuminating'. And then there was the fame. 'If I had been conspicuous in the West Riding,' he wrote, 'I was like a Martian in Cumbria. But a very popular Martian: eyes were always on me on and off the field.'

It is this 192-match spell at Workington, kicked off in season 1953-54 with a try - the first of 55 in total - during a 30-12 debut win at Dewsbury, that is looked back upon fondly by *Open Rugby* founder, *Rugby League Journal* editor and devoted Cumbrian - even if that is primarily with Whitehaven - Harry Edgar.

'Cec truly was a groundbreaker for the people of West Cumberland in the 1950s, because he was the only black man most of them had ever seen in the flesh,' Edgar recalls. 'Apart from other league players like Billy Boston or Johnny Freeman, that is, who would occasionally visit the county with opposing teams. Cec, though, was accepted as one of their own.

'His playing career was just before my time as a young fan, but I knew all about Cec because my father, a keen Workington Town follower and fount of knowledge on all the good things in the game, would talk endearingly about him with a kind of wide-eyed wonderment, and no little pride, that he 'knew' a black man. That was, of course, in addition to his unbridled admiration for Cec as a talented and whole-hearted second-row-forward. Initially he was a capture by Cumberland's hero, Gus Risman, and eventually became a key figure in the Workington side coached by Jim Brough that went to both the Challenge Cup and Championship finals in consecutive weeks in 1958.'

It was at Workington, said Cec in paying tribute to player-coach Risman, that his game really began to blossom. 'His presence had a tremendous influence on me because he always led by example,' Cec wrote. 'Indeed, Gus is my ideal of what a professional games player should be, intelligent, dignified and with no nonsense about him.' Cec also recalled an exchange with Risman while still at Hunslet, when the visitors had been narrowly beaten:

> 'You're a newcomer to the game, aren't you?' he asked.
> 'This is my third season, but I suffered a broken leg in my first,' I replied.
> 'I was very impressed,' said Gus. 'Keep it up.'
> 'Thank you,' I answered. 'I'll try.' I felt elevated; I felt as if God had spoken to me.

In October 1955, after an injury to Sol Roper, Cec was actually named captain. Said one newspaper report: 'Sepia-skinned Cec Thompson, wise in the ways of field craft and master of the delayed pass, put the only polish on to this roughly hewn game. Workington had the ideas, Cec saw to that. Indeed, the Workington skipper set a fine example by his inspiring leadership.'

To a modern eye these patronising and unnecessary references to Thompson's colour and the nickname 'Darkie' that followed him up to Cumbria are cringe-worthy, but in the 1950s the sobriquet went unquestioned, put down by

Harry Edgar to naïveté. 'It was given in a spirit of innocent admiration by a Cumbrian public who took him to their hearts,' he says. 'They recognised his qualities as a man, not just a rugby player.

'They would see him cleaning windows during the week, and then as a champion in the blue and white on Saturday afternoons. My father knew, as did everyone in West Cumberland, about Cec's difficult upbringing - it was the first time I ever heard the word 'orphanage' - and there was widespread admiration for how he was trying to educate himself by learning to read and write enough to the point where, within a few short years, he was Cumberland's popular representative as a columnist in rugby league magazines and newspapers.'

IT was a feeling of warmth that Cec Thompson was happy to reciprocate. Even as his playing career came to an end and new challenges in business - that one-man window cleaning round eventually becoming a money-spinning many-handed organisation, with Cec as its managing director - teaching and studying lay ahead, he never cut his ties with the county, making a home near Cockermouth.

His last game, when it came, was at Bradford, won 28-2, in September 1960. Though first and foremost a second-rower, he'd also played twenty-two games for Workington at loose forward and six matches on the wing. But by now a less physically demanding future was on his mind.

That entry into rugby league journalism improved his literacy skills no end, introducing the idea that perhaps a career might be forged away from manual labour. His hectic spell coaching at Barrow taught him man-management and how to sidestep dinosaur directors, along with juggling the demands of several enterprises, the cleaning business into which he had invested his rugby earnings already a going concern by now, complete with reliant employees and a dodgy business partner. He belatedly took an English 'O' Level at Workington Tech and began a correspondence course, intending one day to be a full-time student and PE teacher.

The first ambition came to pass in 1962, with a four-year college course at what is now the University of Huddersfield. After his marriage to Barbara broke up, he shook off the divorce with a course in physiotherapy. Now familiar with places like Grasmere, Thirlmere, Windermere and Rydal Water, he grew fond of poetry and immersed himself in books. And during the Christmas holidays of 1957, he met his beloved and steadfast wife Anne, with whom he shared the rest of an eventful life that, though far happier, also included spells on the verge of mental breakdown.

And through it all, it was Anne who, according to Harry Jepson, became the engine in his motor: 'She was a school meals supervisor and, when he met her, it was the making of him,' Harry says. 'Anne encouraged him to pursue an education.'

In short, Cec then was gravitating away from rugby league though, in time, he would return, first as the driving force behind Student RL - in the days when such an organisation was unthinkable if not, in some places, banned outright - and still later as a director of the ill-fated club Mansfield Marksman [sic].

Remarried in 1964 while in his second year studying at Huddersfield, after struggling through there he began and completed a further three-year honours degree in economics at Leeds University that would eventually lead to a diploma in education and, after many a stressful year (particularly for Anne, who also gave birth to a son) teaching jobs at

Dinnington High comprehensive and Chesterfield Grammar where, over a 17-year stay, he built a reputation as a hard taskmaster, fought off a false charge of assault and finished up Head of Economics and master of rugby. Oh, and when he got around to selling his cleaning business in 2002, it had a labour force in the hundreds. Phew!

In 1994, Cec Thompson was also awarded an honorary master's degree by Leeds University for services to the community. From a man who couldn't sign his own name when we came in, it had been quite some journey.

But rewind to 1967 and it was at that very seat of learning in Leeds where the route back into rugby league began, when Cec chanced upon Andrew Cudbertson, a chemistry student from Hull, or rather the other way around.

Soon, Leeds SRLC were joining the Hunslet District League, complete with players from China, Africa, America, Australia, New Zealand and Canada, initially taking some hammerings. The historic first recorded Inter-Varsity rugby league match came one year later, on 15 March 1968, when Leeds played Liverpool at Widnes (although there were rumours of vague distant activity in Portsmouth also).

Dave Hadfield's book *Learning Curve* (2013) tells the full remarkable story of the student game in a manner more entertaining and in-depth than we have space for here. And Cudbertson recalls in an interview in its pages the day he asked Cec to coach the team: 'Despite being the hardest-working student I'd ever seen, he agreed.'

Hadfield, meanwhile, goes on to describe that decision as '...the equivalent of the university football club being coached by one of England's World Cup-winning squad of a few months previously; the sort of thing that happens informally but frequently in rugby league and rather less often in other codes.'

Another Hullensian, former RFL Secretary/Chief Executive, recent RFL President, Life Member of the RL Council and much, much else besides, David Oxley CBE, now 77, has his own memories of: '...one of the most remarkable men I have been privileged to meet.'

Speaking in July 2014, a day before nipping off to watch the Students play the Armed Forces in Widnes, in the final stages of the newly-minted Association Cup made up of representative sides from Great Britain Armed Forces, Great Britain Police, Great Britain Teachers and Great Britain Students, the ever loquacious one-time Student Rugby League chairman explained: 'The student game is played everywhere now from Exeter to Aberdeen and all points between, including Ireland and Wales, but that wasn't the case at the start when Cec first came into the picture at Leeds. And as the organisation grew over the years, he was always a keen supporter. He became its vice-president, attended matches with Anne and was always a welcome presence and wonderfully entertaining speaker.

'I first met Cec via the Student Rugby League when I arrived in rugby league in 1974, at Chapeltown Road. As a Hull KR fan, I remembered him as a player, of course. He was one of those who you would shout at as he destroyed your forwards - a very strong man who also tore it up out wide - but the sort who you would have secretly liked in your team.

'He made a big impression in person too. Cec was such a positive force, a very strong character with a great sense of humour and deep humility. He was a man of vision and ideas; it was very sad how he faded late in life.'

Sadly, in his twilight years, Cec Thompson fell victim to dementia, a cruel condition at the best of times, but a particularly sad fate in someone of such drive and indefatigability. He stopped recognising people and his memory slipped. Dementia also worsens gradually, so he nevertheless continued to turn up at rugby league events as before, though with nothing like the same touchline impact or frequency.

'It was a sad sight,' says David Oxley. 'He'd had such an impish sense of fun and was an enormous flirt, in the nicest way. He was a good-looking man and the ladies loved him. Cec made a vibrant impression on everyone he met, which was invaluable for us in future years. We took Cec all over at the RFL and he was very willing to come along and champion the sport.

'There's no doubt his early troubles helped to form his personality. He was one of those who just belong in rugby league and admitted that without it he could have easily gone the wrong way. He'd had no formal education, lived in Hunslet, was seen as illegitimate and grew up around some pretty dodgy elements. He used to say that the game made him, though he in turn put an awful lot into it. Rugby league owes him an enormous amount.'

Not that the ghosts of the past were ever completely exorcised. Doubt and insecurity were constant companions, sparked most frequently by small-mindedness and petty malevolence in people who really ought to have known better. But by Cec's own account his rise through society did at least give him the confidence to stand his ground in any company, however superficially intimidating.

To quote Willis Hall again:

> There is nothing nicer than to have lunch with Cec and to talk until the cows come home about rugby league, literature, society, music, the theatre, politics, art, philosophy - you name it.

13 Inspirations

It was hard to get a word in edgeways, Hall wrote. But the final say, of course, should indeed go to Cec himself.

'Opportunity, wherever it lies, should not be wasted and talent in its many forms often hides within the most improbable people and unlikely circumstances,' he concludes, in the book outlining his life and times.

Born on the 'wrong side' Cec Thompson might well have been, but there is no doubt he lived and ended it on exactly the right one. Ours.

● Tony Hannan is an author, publisher and editor-at-large of *Forty-20*. His rugby league books include *Tries and Prejudice*, the autobiography of Ikram Butt, England's first rugby international in either code, and the biography *Being Eddie Waring*. He once scored a try against Hugh Gumbs.

5. The Father of International RL

John Coffey QSM

IN the early months of 1907, Albert Henry (Bert) Baskerville was a popular young man employed in the Wellington Post and Telegraph office. Humble and polite, he hardly seemed to be the rebellious type. On summer Saturdays he enjoyed success as a middle distance runner and during the winter months he blended size, speed and versatility to perform with distinction at loose forward or in the three-quarters for the Oriental club's senior rugby team.

Because of his family situation, and the lifestyle of the times in what was still a very new and isolated colony, Baskerville would have been expected to spend his entire working life in the employ of the New Zealand Government, while assisting his widowed mother and younger brothers and sisters to recover from the premature death of his father.

But Baskerville was frustrated by a country upbringing which required him to leave school at 13 and denied him university, business and travel opportunities. At 24 years of age he was skilled at Morse code but felt his natural talents were being wasted. The uninspiring routine of his job, however, did not suppress his imagination or ambition.

'He was a masterful man with big ideas,' said renowned rugby union forward William (Massa) Johnston, who was to become a double international when he toured with Baskerville's pioneering All Golds. 'Wearing his life out in the routine of a Government job must have chafed and hurt. A man like that always feels he must "do something".'

Baskerville loved writing. He contributed articles to New Zealand and English newspapers and penned what was acclaimed as the first important book on New Zealand rugby football tactics and methods. Ironically, it was not published until Baskerville had been disqualified for life by the New Zealand Rugby Union and warned off its playing fields. Yet the book still received rave reviews.

Uppermost in Baskerville's mind was the welfare of his family. Tragedy had struck in 1903 when Bert's father was killed when a drain he was digging collapsed on him. At 20, Bert became the breadwinner and when a work promotion transferred him from Auckland to Wellington he took his mother, Maria, and six siblings with him. Most of his income as a postal clerk was directed into the family funds.

Not all of Baskerville's writing was for public consumption. After meeting with members of the 1905-06 All Blacks rugby union team which had toured Britain, he took an increasing interest in the fledgling Northern Union which had broken away from the autocratic England Rugby Union in 1895, and whose players had been prevented from playing the All Blacks. He began corresponding with the Northern Union, proposing a privately-organised tour.

Rumours of a New Zealand team being assembled to play the clubs and counties in the north of England had been circulating for some time, and prominent players throughout the country were threatened with suspensions by the NZRU if they did not sign declarations of amateurism and loyalty.

But it was not until late May 1907 - some months after Baskerville first contacted Northern Union secretary Joe Platt - that NZRU officials identified their man. Baskerville was summoned by the union's management committee - the sporting equivalent of appearing before the Inquisition - to reveal all he knew of 'the proposed tour of professional footballers to England'.

Baskerville's written reply revealed he had already burned his bridges: 'Your union will no doubt gain all the information that I have regarding the proposed tour of "All Black" professional footballers to England in the daily papers in the course of the next few weeks. Until then, I am bound not to divulge it. I severed my connection with the Oriental Football Club on the 25th inst., and am also leaving the Postal Department - A H Baskiville, Hon. Secretary N.Z. Rugby Football Club.'

Baskerville's brief letter had hardly reached NZRU headquarters before the management committee not only disqualified him from any further association with the game but ordered all district rugby unions to prevent him from entering football grounds under their control. The influential NZRU also contacted city and town councils, insisting they enforce the 'Baskiville ban' on their public parks.

(Whether Bert's surname should be spelt Baskiville or Baskerville troubled researchers for decades. Bert's grandfather was actually born Walter Baskival in County Mayo, Ireland, in 1807, but during a 24-year stint in the British army it became Baskivill because of common usage. The next generation altered it to Baskiville and Bert's mother, brothers and sisters kept that. Baskiville is also the spelling on Bert's grave in Wellington's Karori cemetery. But in adulthood Bert wanted to be known as Baskerville, in his various sports, his writings, and his signature. The family believes Bert made the change when first contemplating a trip to England, where Baskerville was the common spelling. It was clearly his preference and most historians now respect that.)

Provincial rugby unions rubber-stamped the ban on the now admitted 'professional' tour organiser and warned any players who had not signed the NZRU loyalty contract that they would also risk their team-mates' amateur status if they played alongside them. Some local bodies at least went through the motions of discussing the situation. Typical was a reported meeting of the Petone Borough Council in Baskerville's Wellington home town.

'Has he killed anyone?' asked Councillor Castle when the Wellington Rugby Union asked the council to warn Baskerville off the Petone Recreation Ground.

'No,' answered the Mayor, 'but I believe he has grievously offended the Rugby Union.'

Councillor Coles: 'I don't think it has anything to do with us. Let them do their own dirty work.'

Councillor Nicholson: 'Can we do anything? It is a free ground.'

Councillor Lodder: 'The union has no power to do anything like that on our grounds.'

Councillor Coles: 'What have we to do with this matter? Is it anything to do with us if he refused to sign a certain paper?'

The Mayor: 'If we liked to write to the Rugby Union authorising them to order the man off they could do so.'

Councillor Lodder: 'Is this matter all there is against the man?'

The Mayor: 'I understand he is the secretary of the New Zealand professional rugby football team.'

Councillor Coles: 'He has admitted it.'

The Mayor: 'If the council is desirous of putting down professionalism in football, now is the chance to show its hand.'

Councillor Castle: 'Who is to say where professionalism begins?'

Councillor Southgate: 'What about putting down professionalism in the union itself? It is after money all the time.'

Councillor Lodder: 'Not individually.'

After the Mayor reminded the meeting the trotting club had been given the power to reserve the right of entry, the council allowed the Rugby Union similar authority. Although most of the quoted councillors obviously had doubts about banning Baskerville, they buckled under when the Mayor raised the bogey of professionalism. So Baskerville was outlawed along with any horse racing fixers and illegal bookmakers previously disqualified by the trotting club.

Ironically, Petone was to be a rich recruiting area for Baskerville. Team manager Harry Palmer was a prominent businessman in the district and tour captain Hercules (Bumper) Wright had led both the Petone club and Wellington provincial teams for the previous four years. A number of other Petone players also joined up.

During the next year the humble postal clerk became the father of international rugby league, introducing what had been a regional sport in England to the winter sports scenes in Australia and New Zealand. Tragically, the title was soon to become posthumous, for Baskerville died from pneumonia in Brisbane during the final leg of the famed nine-month All Golds tour. He was still only 25 years of age.

One must admire Baskerville's courage in taking on the omnipotent NZRU at a time when rugby was enjoying a surge of support from national Government, regional councils and all newspapers because of the achievements of the 1905-06 All Blacks, who lost just one of their 35 games in Britain. Their achievements had taken the country by storm, with crowds forming outside post offices and newspaper buildings waiting for telegraphed news of their latest games to be received from Britain.

But Baskerville was aware that many of the All Blacks players had not been happy with their lot. They had sacrificed much to fill the NZRU coffers with £13,000, but many of them were left broke and unemployed. He knew they referred to themselves as 'three bob a day men' in reference to their miserable daily allowance of three shillings. Some All Blacks had seen Northern Union matches and appreciated not only the permitted 'broken time' payments but also the rule variations which made the game more attractive to players and spectators.

Among those disgruntled players was George Smith, who shared Baskerville's interests in athletics and rugby. Smith still ranks as one of New Zealand's greatest all-round sportsmen. From a horse racing family, he was a New Zealand Cup-winning jockey as a youngster. As an athlete Smith won many national sprint championships, broke a world hurdles record in Melbourne and competed in England. A prolific try-scoring wing, he had been an automatic All Blacks selection since 1897.

Smith had many sporting contacts in Australia and

was aware of the simmering discontent in Sydney rugby circles, where representative players received meagre expenses for travelling inter-state and injured players were not compensated for lost wages. Once it became evident there were sufficient 'rebels' willing to forego their amateur status, Sydney was destined to be the first stop-over for Baskerville's British-bound team.

What originally sparked Baskerville's interest? In 1946 one of Baskerville's brothers, Bill, told a story of how a fellow Wellington postal employee, known only as 'old Harry', suffered a coughing seizure and collapsed to the floor while reading a copy of the *Manchester Evening News*. Once the ailing Harry had been attended to, Bert Baskerville's attention was drawn to a story of big crowds and lucrative gate receipts at Northern Union games.

Baskerville's own version, written from Colombo in 1907 - where the All Golds played a Ceylon team under rugby union rules - differed. The newspaper he mentioned was the *Daily Mail*, and an article written by F W Cooper, who contended the All Blacks had 'not played the cream of English football - such men play under the banner of the Northern Union.' It served as a challenge to Baskerville.

'From a conversation with a returned 1905 All Black, I gleaned that the Northern Union authorities had actually held out a substantial guarantee for a match with the New Zealanders, but of course the match could not be entertained then. That set me thinking why shouldn't a New Zealand team play the Northern Unionists? Guarded conversations with prominent New Zealand players elicited information that, with few exceptions, they would be willing to join a team if one was formed with that purpose in view: so I set to work,' wrote Baskerville.

The NZRU even involved the New Zealand

Government's office in London in a bid to stop the tour of the 'professional All Blacks'. But that was hardly surprising because the London-based Agent General, Cecil Wray Palliser, was also New Zealand's delegate to the (English) Rugby Football Union. Palliser used his contacts at *The Times* in London to issue statements labelling the tourists a 'phantom team', claiming Baskerville was 'hoodwinking the people' and saying the players 'would bring no credit to New Zealand'. But Palliser's outbursts failed to convince Northern Union officials to withdraw their support for the tour.

Newspapers in New Zealand were also scathing in their attacks of Baskerville's activities. The *Evening Post* in Wellington said 'the pro Blacks - a contingent of New Zealand professional footballers - are to sail for Australia, where they are to engage in combat with other leopards who have changed their spots.'

The *New Zealand Times* quoted Auckland Rugby Union president A E Devory as expressing 'regret at the appearances of professionalism in football in this colony. Its evil effects are so well known that it has small chance of obtaining a place among players generally, or with those having control of the game in New Zealand.' Even the Anglican Bishop of Auckland was congratulated by rugby union officials for stating he was 'glad that the battle against professionalism in football was being fought so well.'

Professionalism in sport was regarded as only slightly less desirable than the black plague in the early days of the twentieth century. When rugby league was seeking to establish itself in the wake of the All Golds tour, primary school pupils were threatened with life bans if they embraced the new game. Protestations that the only player payments would be modest allowances to compensate them and their families for lost wages while on tour fell on deaf ears. It seemed that three

Modern-day inspirations: Adrian Morley, Kevin Sinfield and Jamie Peacock, *right*

Mighty respect: Morley and Peacock, *above*, after the Tetley's Challenge Cup final at Wembley stadium in 2012

SWpix.com

Fighting talk: Matt King meets Sam Tomkins during the Gillette Four Nations in 2011... and chats with Jamie Jones-Buchanan, *right*

SWpix.com; Rugby League World

Pioneer: The great Cec Thompson with wife Anne, *above right*, was the first black Englishman to play for Great Britain

War hero: Clark (*front, second right*) with the 352 Siege Battery Ammunition Column

Heavy man: Douglas Clark, *left*, with Ben Gronow. *Right*: 'The Backbone of Britain'

Huddersfield Foundation

Team of All Talents: Huddersfield's all-conquering superstars of 1914-15

THE "ALL GOLDS."

The movement of the "All Golds"—the "Sydney Morning Herald" is the author of the brilliant phrase—seems to have taken a hold in Sydney. According to this paper, the leaders are quite confident that professionalism in Rugby has come to stay. They are careful to make it clear that their professionalism will be much superior to the professionalism at Home, where a man lives by the game. It is intended to insure players against accident, paying their playing and training expenses, and "perhaps make them a bonus at the end of the season, according to results." It is claimed that under such an arrangement the players will be no more professionals than Australian international cricketers, and that they will be doing openly far less than is being done now by so-called amateurs. Playing for the love of playing seems to be a motive of decreasing force. "Not that the boys want to be paid for their Saturday afternoon's fun; but they think, and rightly so, too, that as they draw the crowd they should get something out of the gate money." So said one secretary, who complained bitterly that the player received beggarly compensation for his expenses, his hard knocks, and his more serious injuries. Another secretary laughed rudely at an interviewer who asked him what he thought of the new movement. "Why, bless my soul! You are green! That's no new movement. We've had professionalism in Sydney football for years. Everybody knows it. All the club officials know it; the Union knows it, but they can't prove it, and to save trouble they don't try, much. Why, nearly every club pays directly or indirectly for the services of one or two men every Saturday. And I don't blame them." For instance, a club knows of a first-class forward, who, being a butcher or a grocer, cannot play on Saturday afternoons. The club pays a man to take his place in the shop on those afternoons, so that the forward can play. Some players receive ten shillings for a game. Of course, no receipts are given. There was a recent case in which a club short of forwards tried to induce two men from another club to come over. The players said they would come if they could get good jobs in the district, and work was secured for them at an advance of 7s a week on the wages they were earning. At the last moment they backed out, giving the significant explanation that they were better off where they were. "Who was going to pay that 7s? The club, of course."

Paying their respects: The 1924 Great Britain party visits the grave of Albert Baskerville, father of international rugby league, at Karori cemetery, Wellington   *John Coffey*

Woman in a man's world: Kay Ibbetson pictured in Paris with the East Hull open-age team she took on a five-day tour to France in May, 1963

Victoria Dawson

Determined soul: The late great Steve Prescott MBE enjoys a glass of Champagne at the Old Trafford finishing line on the fourth day of the Steve Prescott Engage Mutual Running Challenge in 2010. *Inset*: Former team-mate Jon Wilkin

SWpix.com

ENGLAND'S RUGBY LEAGUE TEAM

'England' expects: Welshman Trevor Foster leads the charge in this Aussie newspaper cartoon depicting the arrival of the Great Britain Indomitables' in 1946

Battler of Brisbane: Alan Prescott relaxes with his GB caps, *above right*, - including one for his efforts in the 1958 Test down under when he played despite a broken arm. *Below*: Taking to the field in the company of team-mate Alex Murphy   *Saints Heritage Society*

Men of the match: A group of star Challenge Cup finalists gather in 2007 - all of them having won the award named as a tribute to former Wigan player - and much else - Lance Todd, *pictured right*

rlphotos.com

Bowing out: The amazing Darren Lockyer in 2011

COPE'S "CLIPS" CIGARETTES

No. 283.—TODD
Wigan
Noted Footballers

Refusal to be beaten: Mike Gregory and team-mates celebrate with the Lancashire Cup after Warrington's victory over Oldham in the 1989 final

rlphotos.com

shillings per day for an All Black was acceptable; a marginally larger amount for an All Gold was taboo.

That stigma was attached to rugby league for decades and used by rugby unions and city councils to lock the gates of the country's main stadiums - Eden Park in Auckland, Lancaster Park in Christchurch, Wellington's Athletic Park and Dunedin's Carisbrook - whenever requests were made to play fixtures against teams from Australia and Great Britain. Yet England's professional cricketers were always welcomed onto those same grounds.

Baskerville had no-one to fight publicly at his side. There were no administrators to back him up, no rugby league writers on the influential newspapers to put his side of the case. The increasing number of players who encouraged him to remain staunch in the face of all the criticism had themselves to remain anonymous or be disqualified forever from amateur sport.

While Baskerville was the prime target of those who sought to crush his plans, newspapers kept digging away to find out which of the country's leading players were signing on for the supposed 'phantom' team. George Smith was Baskerville's right-hand man in Auckland and kept in touch with his Sydney contacts; manager-elect Harry Palmer and captain-in-waiting Hercules Wright were his lieutenants in Wellington; and flying wing Duncan McGregor, who had scored four tries for the 1905 All Blacks against England at Crystal Palace, was the main man in Christchurch.

By coincidence or not, the NZRU decided to send an All Blacks touring team to Australia during the 1907 season. One newspaper scribe earned the union's ire by suggesting players could have the best of both worlds by touring Australia as an amateur and then going to England with Baskerville's team. Otago forward Massa Johnston did just that.

13 Inspirations

In early June the *Auckland Star* proclaimed the unsanctioned tour would proceed, the team would be strong, and that Auckland players who had signed the NZRU declaration had done so only after taking legal advice - they were informed there was no legal liability if they subsequently took part in the tour. Over the next two months lists of prospective tourists were published and even if not all reports were totally accurate it was clear that Baskerville was making serious inroads into New Zealand's rugby ranks.

Baskerville's exceptional negotiating skills had given him plenty to bargain with. Although every member of his touring party was required to stump up £50 for preliminary expenses, he virtually guaranteed them a good return on their investment. Northern Union secretary Joe Platt offered Baskerville 70 per cent of every gate and a minimum return of £3,000 so long as he gathered a quality team which included some of the 1905 All Blacks.

It is believed that 140 of the 400 representative players in New Zealand applied to become members of Baskerville's team, including 18 of the 1905 All Blacks. The names of those who missed out - either because they could not raise £50 or were not suited to the new form of rugby which had discarded line-outs and side-row forwards - were kept confidential to protect their amateur status.

George Smith, Duncan McGregor, Massa Johnston and Bill Mackrell were the 1905 All Blacks who went back to Britain. Eric Watkins, Tom Cross, Edgar Wrigley and English-born Hubert (Jum) Turtill had also represented New Zealand. Captain Hercules Wright (so named because he was believed to be the biggest baby born in his district) was one of several regarded as very unlucky not to have been All Blacks.

In August the team left in two groups from Wellington and Auckland, bound for Sydney to start a nine-month odyssey which became one of the most remarkable sporting ventures of all time. Because no-one possessed a rule book or had seen Northern Union in its evolving form - team numbers had been reduced from 15 to 13 since the 1905 All Blacks tour - the three Sydney games were rugby union. The Australian media dubbed them the All Golds, a name which was meant to be derogatory because they were deemed to be professionals, but which now holds a proud place in New Zealand sporting folklore.

While in Sydney, Baskerville was so impressed with outstanding back and goal-kicker Dally Messenger that he recruited him for the British tour. Messenger's switch from rugby union was a major factor when sports fans had to choose which code to follow when the Sydney rugby league premiership began in 1908. The All Golds' share of the gate money from their Sydney games boosted their bank balance and lifted morale for the strenuous itinerary which lay ahead.

Lancashire and Yorkshire had dominated rugby union county championships before the Northern Union breakaway in 1895 and Baskerville never doubted his team would face tougher opposition than that encountered by the 1905 All Blacks against predominantly 'soft' southern teams. Only in working-class Wales had the All Blacks been truly tested, and it was there that they suffered their sole loss.

Curiously, a review of Baskerville's book - titled *Modern Rugby Football (New Zealand methods)* - appeared in the *New Zealand Herald* after the All Golds arrived in England. So effusive is its praise for the author that the reviewer was surely not aware of his blacklisting by every rugby union body in the country.

'It is readily admitted by New Zealand footballers that Mr A H Baskerville is among their leading authorities upon Rugby, as it is played throughout this Dominion. Mr

Baskerville's neat and handy little book, which is excellently printed, bound and illustrated with instructional photographs and diagrams, aims at "explaining the modern game in such a manner that after careful reading a team of fifteen men green to the game could go onto a field and play a game of Rugby football." As might be anticipated from the standing of the writer, the book is not only a valuable teacher, but it will be found highly useful as a reference book, even where the game is played at its best and the methods most generally understood.'

Despite their lack of Northern Union knowledge, the All Golds hit the ground running in Britain. Bramley were beaten 25-6 in the first match between teams from different nations, and only a draw with Wakefield Trinity interrupted eight consecutive victories. But as injuries and illness - especially influenza - reduced the ranks, and the harsh northern winter made it difficult to maintain their free-running style, the losses began to outnumber the wins.

Only one of seven games in January produced a victory, and the defeats included those to Wales (8-9 at Aberdare), an England XIII (16-18 at Wigan) and the Northern Union (6-14 at Leeds) in the first of three Test matches. The tour was to finish with four matches in February, including the last two Tests, but there was relief from an exhausting schedule of playing and travelling. Instead of three games each week, only Saturdays were match days.

There was valuable time to recover and prepare. Northern Union were beaten 18-6 at Chelsea to level the Test series and the All Blacks emerged triumphant 8-5 from a tough decider at Cheltenham. Only then did Baskerville allow himself the luxury of making his playing debut, and he was try-scorer in the tour-ending victory over St Helens. The All Golds had won 19, lost 14 and drawn two of their British fixtures.

Bill Mackrell, having toured Britain with both the All Blacks and All Golds, was adamant which tour was tougher: 'In my opinion, the Northern Union players are streets ahead of the amateurs at Home,' he told the *Auckland Star*. 'They play a game which is miles ahead of the standard rules. For a while we experienced some difficulty in conforming to the Northern Union regulations but once we got into the running we were able to hold our own.

'It was unfortunate that we should have encountered such a wet winter. There seemed to be nothing but rain, hail and fog. Just before the first Test match our men were nearly all down with influenza or colds. None of us were able to train and we were never a hope of winning the match. Afterwards, we managed to regain something like decent health, and had no trouble in winning the next two Tests.'

Mackrell also disclosed that, despite the weather, the tour had been a financial success, with each team member to receive a handsome £300 reward for his initial £50 outlay. (That Baskerville did not use the tour to feather his own nest was revealed after his death, when the Public Trustee's valuation of his assets totalled less than £250).

Massa Johnston said the managerial policies of Harry Palmer had been strict, with one notable exception: 'Even such little things as our comings and goings in the evenings had to be submitted (to Palmer). But Albert Baskerville was always considered to be an exception outside the rule. No one ever thought of questioning what he did or when he came and went.'

Despite being tour organiser, secretary and freelance journalist, Baskerville regularly trained with the team. He was respected by Northern Union officials and his engaging manner enabled him to obtain 'an entrée into very exclusive circles in England'. He had an insatiable appetite for information and was a compulsive note taker. It is believed he would have stayed on in Britain had there not been agreement of an Australian tour on the homeward journey.

Baskerville was meticulous in his handling of the finances. He made a habit of arriving at playing venues hours before kick-off to check facilities, including the turnstiles, and when the first balance sheet was produced in Manchester the auditors made complimentary reference to the business-like manner in which the books had been kept. But it took a toll, according to Johnston.

'When it was all over, and the boys were on the boat leaving England, he just seemed like an old man who had lost interest in the past and was looking far into the future. He told us he already considered the tour a success, and that he was looking forward to taking a team to America - that was to be his next achievement if he could manage it.'

While in England, Baskerville and Northern Union officials discussed the prospects of a reciprocal trip to Australia and New Zealand, laying the foundations for the first Lions tour in 1910. Five of the All Golds backs, including George Smith (Oldham) and Lance Todd (Wigan), remained in Britain at tour's end. With Dally Messenger about to change from valued team-mate to respected rival in the first trans-Tasman Test series, Baskerville relished a chance to become a regular player in Australia.

The inaugural Sydney premiership had not started when the All Golds arrived in April 1908, and they willingly assisted the clubs to learn the laws and tactical nuances of the new rugby. Massa Johnston was adamant Baskerville's sole appearance against St Helens had been so convincing that he earned selection at wing for the first Test against Australia at Sydney's Royal Agricultural Ground entirely on merit. He was to more than justify his inclusion.

During the first half Baskerville intercepted a pass near the halfway line, evaded two opponents with sheer pace, and scored the try which gave New Zealand an 8-0 lead. It was 11-2 at half-time. But Johnston was sent off on a punching charge (later exonerated on a touch judge's report) and the Australians, captained by Messenger, surged back. The All Golds defended desperately over the last 15 minutes to win 11-10.

'The new three-quarter in the team [Baskerville], usually a forward, was the best back on the ground and was indeed the surprise packet of the day,' said one newspaper. The writer went so far as to suggest the New South Wales Rugby League should make Baskerville an offer to stay 'based on the experience he has gained in the executive position and his knowledge as a player - Mr Baskerville would be a valuable man.'

The All Golds set sail for Brisbane to ignite the rugby league flame in Queensland. Several players, including Baskerville, caught influenza on the boat. Baskerville's health deteriorated rapidly and three days later he was admitted to the Victoria private hospital suffering from pneumonia. In an era before antibiotics he was treated with sulphur drugs which failed to arrest his decline.

On Wednesday, May 20, the All Golds beat a Brisbane Metropolitan team before word reached the players that Baskerville was in a precarious condition. Some still in playing gear, they rushed to his bedside and found their inspirational leader unconscious. He died in the early evening.

The whole team wanted to go home immediately, but with obligations to play two more Tests and a return match against Queensland that was not realistic. Baskerville's body was embalmed and placed in a lead casket. Manager Harry Palmer and six players, representing each New Zealand province, accompanied the casket by train to Sydney and then across the Tasman Sea to Wellington on the steamer *Monowai*.

Only 12 players were fit enough to take the field against Queensland. They were held to a draw by a side they had easily beaten a week earlier. But these exhausted men lifted themselves one more time to clinch the Test series with a resounding 24-12 victory at the Brisbane Exhibition Ground. They had conquered both Britain and Australia to become the first international champions of rugby league. After leading 9-3, they eventually sagged to a 9-14 loss in the third Test back in Sydney. It was one match too many. Arrangements had been made to hold the ship so they could finally go home.

There were lavish tributes to Baskerville on both sides of the Tasman from a previously hostile media.

New Zealand Herald (Sydney correspondent): 'From every quarter of Australia messages of sympathy have come to the team, and the deepest condolence with Baskerville's widowed mother and other relatives is also expressed. Amongst the men he fought, the authorities of the Rugby Union, Baskerville was personally very popular, and whilst they opposed him tooth and nail in his big scheme to establish professional football, they recognised the strength with which he fought for the cause he had made his own and the masterful way in which, single-handedly, he brought his scheme to success in spite of the opposition of the ruling football authorities, the press, and a big section of the public. Such a man, had he lived, would have done well.'

The New South Wales and Queensland rugby unions sent wreaths to Baskerville's funeral in Wellington, and flew flags at half-mast at their grounds, gestures which made the total absence of any acknowledgements from the New Zealand and Wellington rugby unions all the more glaring.

Sydney rugby union club games were postponed on a day when a rugby league benefit match was held to assist Baskerville's mother. That did not occur in Wellington, where rugby union club fixtures drew sparse attendances while 8,000 people watched another Baskerville benefit at Athletic Park. All available All Golds played in what was the first rugby league game on New Zealand soil, but the last at Athletic Park for 83 years as union took control of the venue.

New Zealand Herald (Auckland rugby columnist): 'Bert was a young fellow of many sterling qualities. Amongst his companions on and off the field he was a warm favourite, but behind all that there was about his private life real nobility of character that endeared him to his intimates. It may not be generally realised how sad Bert Baskerville's death is, and what a severe blow it will have inflicted upon his widowed mother. Some years ago the deceased's father met with a fatal accident in Auckland. Since that time Bert had devoted himself as few boys do to their mother. Owing mainly to his steady conduct and industrious habits, Mrs Baskerville was able to provide herself with a comfortable home at Kelburn, in Wellington. Bert was her mainstay, however, and the relations between him and his mother were such as to entitle him to the utmost praise. His place in the family circle will leave a pathetic gap.

'No less will Bert's many comrades miss the manly young fellow. The qualities so marked in home life were just as apparent during his athletic career. He was known as a good all-round athlete, being for some time a prominent member of the Oriental club first fifteen. As a runner he was well known as a most generous opponent as well as a desperate finisher, his best performances being done over middle distances. His secretarial abilities were well known, and it has been stated that it was the intention of the promoters of the Australian professional football team to visit

England next season to engage him as secretary. Athletes have been deeply shocked, and the sympathy of every true sport will go out to his relatives in their bereavement.'

The *Auckland Star* also revealed: '...it was intended to have offered [Baskerville] an important managerial position in the NSW professional team to leave for the Old Country in the course of the next few months.' Baskerville and Messenger were to have been reunited on the 1908-09 Kangaroos tour.

Baskerville indisputably founded international rugby league. It was his courage and organisational skills which gave the Northern Union an international credibility at a time when rugby union tours were coming into vogue. He and his men twice provided momentum for the rugby league cause in New South Wales and Queensland. They also passed on their experience to the fledgling Sydney clubs which started what is now the massive NRL premiership. Had Baskerville lived, there is no doubt rugby league would have enjoyed a much stronger foundation and direction in New Zealand. Without him, and in the absence of such strong figures as British-based George Smith and Lance Todd, the remaining All Golds did as much as they could to establish the game in a rugby union-dominated country.

Albert Henry Baskerville was inducted into the New Zealand Sports Hall of Fame in 1996 and the New Zealand RL Legends of League in 2001. It took a letter of enquiry from the NZRL at the time of the All Golds centenary in 2007 to obtain an acknowledgement from the by now very professional NZRU that all life disqualifications had been lifted.

● John Coffey QSM is a long-time New Zealand sports journalist - the only one to tour with 1971's Grand Slam Kiwis in Britain and France. His books include *Being Frank: The Frank Endacott Story* (2002) and (with the late Bernie Wood) *The Kiwis: 100 Years of International Rugby League* (2007).

6. A Fighter Forever

Jon Wilkin

I WALKED into Langtree Park, St Helens, to sign the book of condolences on 10 November 2013.

It was a crisp and calm day, amazingly still and quiet. I wasn't alone, though. A huge gathering had begun to form, full of people who felt proximity and affinity with one man and his struggle. I pondered for a moment what to write. The book lay open in front of me before, thankfully, came a second of absolute clarity: a piece of a poem I'd stuck on my bedroom wall as a kid, that I had drawn comfort from now and again.

Even so, these particular lines had been devoid of real meaning until Steve Prescott passed away the previous day. Just a few words I thought I'd understood, but hadn't really.

Now, in this queue, among people displaying such emotion, those words made perfect sense.

> 'If you can force your heart and nerve and sinew
> To serve your turn long after they are gone,
> And so hold on when there is nothing in you
> Except the Will which says to them: "Hold on!"'

The poem, of course, is *If* by Rudyard Kipling, a famous work that essentially lists the characteristics any good person ought to possess. From my limited understanding of human nature, I believe people have many key qualities, such as patience, honesty and perseverance, for example.

The key quality in the passage above is endurance, the power to endure in what is seemingly a hopeless situation. In 2006, when 'Prekky' was first informed of the extent of his illness, he made the decision to look the endless pain, chronic fatigue, mental torture, extreme stress and adversity that life had, cruelly, already begun to throw at him right in the eye. Who among us knows how we would react when given news of a stomach ridden with cancerous tumours and no chance of survival. Steve stood tall. And he continued to maintain that same positive mindset over the majority of what turned out to be his last seven years.

His was an inspirational approach then, and one that spoke to me of human spirit, of this in-built desire to survive that we all have but which is very often buried beneath the layers of everyday modern living. It spoke of an ability to endure pain and fatigue and do so in a stoic manner; to get up, dust yourself off and just crack on with things.

Steve took this attitude to the extreme and in doing so set an example that shouldn't be ignored. His determined endurance made Steve Prescott MBE a true motivating force for anyone who took the time to hear and understand his story. He certainly fired a burning spark in me.

STEVE's story is now well-documented, not least in his 2014 autobiography published posthumously, *One in a Million: My Story*, written in association with the author Mike Critchley and completed upon Steve's death by his wife, Linzi.

A future St Helens, Hull, Wakefield, Great Britain and Ireland full-back, he was a talented young man, that much is for sure, a gifted sportsman with a fine pedigree to boot. Football and rugby league were his disciplines of choice until, inevitably as it now seems, in 1992 his speed and agility were recognised by one of the loves of his life - and one of the loves of my life - *our* team, his hometown club St Helens.

Steve's dad, Eric, had been a professional rugby league player himself, with St Helens, Salford and Widnes. Steve inherited that natural ability and the road was now clear for his journey into professional sport.

Every player has a visible and stand-out moment during their career and, sat in a living room in Hull, I vividly recall watching Steve Prescott, nasal strip across the brow of his nose, score two fantastic tries in the 1996 Challenge Cup final win over Bradford Bulls at Wembley - he should have scored a third! - a feat of achievement of which most players can only dream. That exceptional 1996 Saints team played their part in one of the most memorable finals in Challenge Cup history and, with Steve at the heart of it all, carved their names in sporting history.

As a young fan, I loved watching Steve play. His pace was exceptional and his ability to anticipate space and inevitably burst through it defined his exceptional talents. Following an equally successful 1996 club campaign in which Saints became the first ever Super League champions, he was chosen to play for England and a dream really had come true. He played in both games during a successful European Championship campaign, scoring three tries and kicking seven goals. The following year, he was part of the powerhouse Saints side that retained the Challenge Cup, once more against that year's eventual champions Bradford. Adversity, though, would now start to be a familiar feature.

On the whole, that 1997 domestic season turned out to be an injury-ravaged one. By the end of it, he was sold to Hull, a genuine low at the time but, as was his style, a move turned ultimately to his advantage. Troughs as well as peaks are part of a career in elite professional sport, those ebbs and flows are something that every single athlete has to go through. Not all of us, though, endure them with quite so much positivity as Steve did. At Hull for a couple of years, then Wakefield, the club he departed to and then went back to Hull from once the Wildcats ran into financial difficulties, he was not only fantastically popular, but hugely successful too. As Steve grew more experienced, that youthful pace was matched by a broader understanding of the game and greater positional sense. As a result he enjoyed representative honours for Lancashire and switched allegiances to Ireland during this period also, representing the Emerald Isle in the 2000 Rugby League World Cup.

In fact, it was while on the representative stage - with Lancashire in Origin in 2003 - that he suffered the serious knee injury which prematurely brought the curtain down on a glorious career. Steve Prescott had been an outstanding rugby league player, out of the top drawer, a fact too often overlooked in and among all the praise that would come his way during the fight to come. He battled his way through every match and extracted every ounce of talent out of his relatively diminutive frame. And when time was called on his on-field exploits, by which point he had scored exactly 999 domestic points, Steve departed the stage as an articulate, outwardly confident guy who knew the trappings of success but who had also known failure.

Professional sporting careers can be volatile things, a fact that myself am very familiar with, as is anyone who plays. But without doubt, those ups and downs armed Steve with the weapons he would need to tackle the issues that began to come to light not long after his playing retirement. The highs and lows of sport force you to deal with negativity and feedback in the most unnatural way. Rugby league players are programmed not to show any weakness or pain. We are constantly faced with and told about our own faults and have to come up with practical ways of fixing them, day in and day out. As the ultimate professional, Steve, as I'm sure his team-mates at Saints, Hull and Wakefield would testify, was exceptional at all of that.

The story of each of our lives meanders through a series of defining moments, and in this at least Steve was no exception.

About to move into his third decade, though still at a relatively young age, Steve may well have believed that his most breathtaking achievements and challenges had been and gone when that injury came in 2003. Yet nothing could have been further from the truth.

The defining point in his life was yet to come, the day in September 2006 when he was diagnosed with a rare form of stomach cancer: pseudomyxomaperitonea. Heartbreakingly, he was told he had just six months to live and that he would not see his children, Taylor and newborn Koby, grow up.

It was now that the incentivising philosophy began. Christmas 2006 was used as a carrot to inspire hope and a date that he could aim to survive until. I have tried to put myself in Prescott family's shoes at this time but it is beyond my contemplation the range of emotions and uncertainty that must have filled both Linzi and Steve's minds as young parents, not to mention husband and wife.

As anyone would, Steve and Linzi reacted in shock and disbelief. But thanks largely to an intervention from Steve Crooks, a friend and coach at Hull FC, another flame was ignited and the word 'inspiration' again becomes relevant, as it would do ever afterwards when thinking about Steve Prescott MBE.

'Why don't you curl up and die then, despite the fact that you have a brand new baby? If you are going to die, then let's have a battle...' - Steve Crooks

We are influenced by the people in our lives and Steve Crooks's call to arms, Prekky's will to survive and his love for his wife and young family were the chief factors behind his fortitude and need to keep his cancer at bay for as long as he possibly could.

Steve never stopped questioning what the authorities in medicine were telling him from day one. He believed he could keep going and studied his own condition in great detail. What's more, he was proved right. By challenging the medical world at every turn, he not only survived for over six years longer than expected, he created a legacy that will now go on to inspire hope and determination in others.

To date, the Steve Prescott Foundation - launched in 2007 - has raised over £500,000 in the pursuit of cures and treatments for cancer through its various fundraising efforts, most of them spearheaded by Steve himself, whatever his state of health at the time, leading to the awarding of an MBE for services to rugby league and charity in the 2010 New Year

Honours list. It has also aided the RFL benevolent fund and the beneficiary of this book, Rugby League Cares.

But the SPF's main asset as we move into the future is a distilled and concentrated dose of Steve Prescott's indomitable personality The foundation continues to portray what the man was all about, facing challenges, overcoming adversity and enduring when your body is simply screaming: 'Give up!'.

During Steve's seven-year battle he led from the front, taking people who thought they were used to withstanding challenges to a point of submission and encouraging them to complete often unimaginable feats of endurance. He didn't just set these challenges, he completed them personally, leaving his doctors, family and everyone around him, myself included, flabbergasted and confused as to how such a terminally ill man could do these things and look so healthy. When he wasn't running in the, say, London Marathon, he was cycling from Land's End to John O'Groats, while completing the National Three Peaks Challenge en route.

Marginally less tiring were a host of charity boxing tournaments - fighting coming naturally, it seems, to a bloke born on Boxing Day - and rugby league matches, with a number of Prekky's former team-mates taking part.

The SPF foundation continues to push boundaries and I have no doubt that Steve will be looking on full of pride at what he has created. He will also most likely be poking holes into it all, enquiring as to why things aren't even bigger and better, but that was just the way he was.

Years passed and through his own research and perseverance Steve did finally find a surgeon and place that could help him. As a result, at the Churchill Hospital in Oxford, he underwent a pioneering first-in-the-world modified multi-visceral transplant, including his stomach, pancreas, small intestine and abdominal wall. It was an operation that intended to remove the cancer from his stomach for good. Steve survived the surgery, but the procedure took a gruelling 32 hours and it was actually complications after the operation that put an end to Steve's fight. But what a fight he had shown.

Cancer is a brutal and awful disease that consumes the people it afflicts. I went to visit Steve in Oxford with Paul Wellens prior to him finding a donor and was overwhelmed by the changes the disease was making to his body. Visibly, he looked as ill as I had ever seen him. I felt really sad coming away from the hospital that day but, despite my own selfish feelings of pity for this man, he was not bothered one bit. He was not consumed by the disease. He appeared as resilient and positive as he'd always been.

The final time I saw Steve, he had climbed on the exercise bike in his room with the aim of knocking out a few kilometres, to keep him in good nick for the operation.

Just staggering.

INITIALLY, when asked to write down some thoughts about Steve Prescott as a figure of inspiration and motivation, I was daunted at the prospect.

Firstly, I only knew Steve *quite* well, not in enough depth to analyse his character in the depth that a good mate or family member could. But when I went to the keyboard, I started in what I thought was the most logical place and looked up the word 'inspiration'. Doing that quickly made me realise that a single word - inspiration - and simple definition just wasn't going to be enough.

A word can't do justice to the multitude of physical reactions, feelings, emotions and actions that can come about due to somebody becoming inspired by someone else. I am unsure about whether, right at the start, Steve set out to be an inspiration to people, or if deep down following his diagnosis he became acutely aware of a responsibility or chance to light up peoples' senses and drive.

I am unsure whether Steve, via his spirit, set out to lead people down a path where self-pity is absent, where endurance and stoicism rules, where ego and self-interest are not welcome.

Yet whether it was an unintended consequence or not, the fact remains that his time on this earth touched peoples' lives in many ways and, in many cases, left a mark that remains on me and some of my closest friends.

Inspiration and motivation can come from the darkest places and in the darkest times of your life, or they can come from the most positive moments. Inspiration can come from people you know and people you don't. It can come from things you see , hear and imagine. Inspiration and motivation are also about challenging what is widely considered to be normal, and silencing that little voice inside you that holds you back when you creep into unknown territory.

There is just no escaping the fact that cancer is a disease that will affect us all during our lives in one way or another. Only Steve honestly knew the pain he felt and the urges he no doubt had to wallow in occasionally, tempting him to seek pity.

But Prekky chose a different path and, in so doing, showed everyone else the way.

When it appears that all is useless and you are defeated, exhausted and feeling self conscious or vulnerable, think of my mate Steve Prescott MBE and his inspiring tale of overcoming adversity, dealing and living with cancer in a way that made all the trivial bullshit in our lives seem embarrassingly insignificant.

Steve reminded us that challenging yourself is always important and was a reminder of the heights to which the human spirit is capable of reaching. He inspired change in so many people and I know, hand on heart, that Prekky will live on in the minds and hearts of the people he touched. And that is guaranteed to last through the ages now that the annual Super League Man of Steel award will henceforth carry his name.

Steve Prescott MBE wasn't an exceptional guy, he was a normal guy who did exceptional things. RIP Steve.

Jon Wilkin is a professional rugby league player and BBC pundit who, since beginning his career at Hull Kingston Rovers, has gone on to great success with St Helens, England and Great Britain. In 2012, he became the first chairman of League 13 - the Super League Players' Association.

7. 'They've a Girl as Boss...'

Victoria Dawson

IF you could have five people over for dinner, from the past or present, who would you invite and why?

Just about everyone, at some point in their lives, will have played this game. Perhaps you wiled an hour away in the car on the way to Wembley, trying to choose between Marx or Engels, or argued with someone on a coach trip to an away game over which of the 1914 Great Britain team you'd rather converse with and why.

My choices would largely be literary and musical; Christopher Marlowe and Bram Stoker would meet Nina Simone and Lux Interior over a glass of Argentinian Malbec and Mediterranean tapas. However, the seat of honour would be reserved for an ordinary woman from Hull who, I've no doubt, would enchant everyone with her stories of determination and success against the odds.

That woman is Kay Ibbetson.

Kay and I have never met, but we have spent many wonderful days together over the last few years, playing a game of hide and seek. I have chased her through the cobbled streets of Hull's Old Town, cycled with her along Preston Road in the east of the city, and got lost in her shadow on the Bransholme Estate in the north.

The first time I saw Kay was in the summer of 2012, when she waved at me from the pages of *Rugby League Magazine*.

'Scorn and ridicule are generally the just and deserved rewards of women who try to talk Rugby League - a real man's preserve if ever there was one' stung the opening lines of N.R. Maplethorpe. I felt those words cut to the quick; even today when people discover that I research the history of women's involvement in rugby league, I often receive similarly snide comments by way of reply. 'This then must be the measure of Kay Ibbetson's success' Maplethorpe went on, 'to have overcome male prejudice and be accepted as one of them in the amateur Rugby League code'. Wow, I thought. Even today, the formidable Kath Hetherington hasn't been wholly accepted by the game, so how, in 1964, did this woman manage it? Perhaps it was down to the tired eyes of a researcher reading under dim lighting, but with that thought I'll swear I saw her wink at me from the page.

And so it began. Maplethorpe's article was all I had to go on. It told me she was the 35-year-old secretary of East Hull RLFC, and that she was the first woman on the Amateur Rugby League Council; her background was in youth club work and she was a successful businesswoman who ran a clerical agency. She also supported Hull Kingston Rovers, but even though I'm a Hull FC fan I couldn't hold it against her. I had so many questions in my head: how did she cope when she started out with East Hull? What problems did she face? I reckoned she must be about 83, so would I be able to track her down and speak to her? Full of burning excitement, off I went to Hull History Centre in search of Kay.

I squealed with delight when the index of names brought up two entries that led me to newspaper articles from 1961. Astonishingly, Kay made front page news in January 1961 when the *Hull and Yorkshire Times* lauded her as the 'belle of the oval-shaped ball' with the headline 'They've a girl as boss of their rugby team'. Whilst journalist John Rodgers emphasised the masculinity of rugby league, he could not hide his admiration for Kay as he introduced her to the public:

> For a woman, Kay Ibbetson, a tall, attractive, mature redhead, certainly has one of the strangest ambitions - she wants enough money to build a permanent headquarters for a boys' rugby club. Repeat: rugby - that rough, tough game for brawny men. Belle of the oval-shaped ball, Miss Kay is the only female rugby club secretary in the whole of Yorkshire, and her beau is East Hull Rugby League FC. A woman who can control 35 lusty, high-spirited youths, and silence the sniggers of rival males, must have some fine qualities, but it is surprising not to find her as large and tough as a Sherman tank.

Kay, embroiled in a man's world, married to the club, may not have been built like a tank but it seemed that she very much had the drive of one.

Firm but Fair

IT all started for Kay while she was involved in youth club work at Maybury Road Youth Club in East Hull, and in 1958, realising that the club did not have a rugby league team, she set one up. However, the team were expelled from the club for a misdemeanour involving alcohol.

Kay, a singular woman who advocated discipline, strongly believed the punishment was too severe. Convinced of the social benefits of rugby league for young boys, she backed her team, saying 'rather than let these boys be without any guidance or interest, I resigned and formed a club for them'. Resigning from the youth club meant that Kay not only had to organise the team, but train them too, something unheard of for a woman at the time. She was very knowledgeable about the game, and preferred a fast, open style of rugby; the type of rugby she enjoyed to watch. In later years she spoke fondly of how she used to pass the ball around and was proud of doing so.

At the same time, over at Craven Street Youth Club, a battle was going on over who would take charge of the Championship winning under-17s side the following season.

It was usual for a coach to take on an under-17s side and see them through their under-19s season too, but at Craven Street, under-17s coaches Dennis Laws and Fred Whittaker had something of a bust up with the under-19s coach Bill Robinson, because Bill wanted to take the under-19s team again after his boys had progressed to open age. Bill had apparently done this before, but this time, Dennis stood his ground.

He had built his team well, and had players like

'Flash' Flanagan, Bob Coverley, Alan Burwell and Ted McNamara playing in his side. Having just won the championship, Dennis did not want to give up his team easily, nor did his team want to leave him.

Assistant Fred Whitaker got in touch with Maybury Youth Club, where Kay had set up her under-17s side, and the Craven Street lads went there to train. The team were all set to transfer to Maybury, but when Alan Burwell and Mike Bullock went to the youth club dance one night, the club told Burwell that he could not come in. Burwell went to Riley High School and the headmaster, having discovered that he planned to attend the dance, had rung the club expressing his wish that Burwell would be denied entry as he should be at home studying for his exams.

To this day Alan has no idea how his headmaster found out he was planning to go to the dance. At the next training session, the captain of the team said that if Burwell wasn't allowed in the youth club then the full team wouldn't be going in again. The transfer to Maybury was off.

With the two youth teams looking for new homes, they joined forces and the new East Hull Rugby League Football Club was born.

Kay was very much the boss, organising everything. As the club's secretary she looked after the club's administration, but Kay was not afraid of hard work and remained very hands on, continuing to coach the younger lads at times.

She was firm, but fair, and joked that everyone knew her as Kay, unless they wanted something, then it was Miss Ibbetson! The teams played at East Park, but Kay had great difficulty in finding the boys somewhere to train. 'I called on every hall in East Hull, but no one wanted 35 lads bouncing on their floors,' she said. Her persistence paid off however, and the vicar of St John's, the Reverend P. Haynes, eventually lent her the use of his hall. However, this was only temporary, and sporadic, so the club had to move about a lot.

Other clubs were suspicious of East Hull for having a woman as a secretary, but Kay shrugged off criticism and pointed to the record of the two teams, which was exemplary. In their first two months the juniors lost only one of five games and were top of the league. The intermediates were unbeaten in nine matches. They even beat the Hull Kingston Rovers B team 36-12; and as Kay said: 'They are professionals getting £2 a match. Our boys pay to play!'

A kindly disciplinarian, she found no difficulty in controlling a large number of boys. She advocated good behaviour on the field, saying:

> Our boys are fairly well-mannered. It doesn't matter what they say in front of me, I've got cloth ears. But I don't like them to swear on the field. It is not sportsmanship. Both our teams play cleanly and, above all, they are enthusiastic. That's what gives me so much heart to do things for them.

Determined to bring some stability to the club, she told the *Hull and Yorkshire Times*: 'Give me five years and I'll have a clubhouse or my name's not Ibbetson.' She was very proud of who she was and clearly good at what she did, because she had a clubhouse in a mere ten months, an achievement which is testament to her dedication and devotion to the club.

Kay was adept at networking and used her business skills to her advantage. Albert Draper, a director at Hull KR, put Kay in touch with a businessman who was willing to let her rent a warehouse in Hedon, a village just to the east of the city. The former grain store had been unoccupied for eight years previously, and when Kay took it on she ignored the rat-infestation and focused on the goal of making it a permanent home for the club.

Kay and the boys set about raising money for refurbishments, and with the generosity of Hull KR, Hull FC and other local businesses, Kay raised a total of £285 for the renovations, which she and the club members mostly did themselves to keep the costs down. Kay described the generosity of local people as 'overwhelming' and they had many donations of furniture and electrical equipment. Someone even gave them a piano.

This restored her 'faith in human nature' as she came in for some criticism, not least from the people of Hedon, who worried that the club may apply for an alcohol license. Her motives however, were purely about social good. East Hull's new headquarters were to be used as a youth club, as Kay wanted somewhere for 'her boys' and girls to relax and take part in normal youth club activities. She said:

> So many youngsters at youth clubs are ham-tied by regulations and red tape and they don't enjoy themselves. Here we want to give them advice rather than authority, and we've built up respect between ourselves and the boys by friendship [...] all of them come to me when they're in trouble or have problems. By giving them responsibility and letting them virtually build this clubhouse themselves, we've something to be proud of, and it means a lot more to them than a clubhouse they could just walk straight into.

A successful open age side was developed that season, and East Hull became a breeding ground for talent; players from the club that went on to become professionals included Hull's

13 Inspirations

Trevor Carmichael and Roger Booth and Hull KR's John Moore and Alan Burwell. Kay cared about the team beyond the playing of the game and used her professional experience to help many an East Hull graduate negotiate their first professional contract.

Scent of a Woman

KAY IBBETSON was not one to settle - it seems that she was always striving to push the club forward.

In May 1963, Kay facilitated a five day trip to France for the open age team, making East Hull the first Yorkshire amateur club to play international football.

Matches were arranged against a Paris XIII and the semi-professional Regiment de Jonville, a side made up of members of the French Army. For many an East Hull player, this was a first trip abroad or at least on an aeroplane. For Kay, arranging the trip wasn't always easy and, as her friend Julie Dunham would later tell me, she met with some opposition because 'she was a [single] woman going away with men.'

In the first match, East Hull were beaten 14-12 by the Paris Selection XIII. Mike Bullock, who had been with East Hull since the Craven Street days, later recalled that the game was played in torrential rain and the mud was so thick the players could hardly lift their feet off the ground. They were ahead at half-time, but with only one substitution facing a fresh set of forwards in the second half, they did well to keep the score tight and even had a match-winning try disallowed at the close of game.

The East Hull team were recognised all over Paris and

treated like film stars. Mike recalled that waitresses in cafés would come up and talk to them about the matches, and one lad even got his studs put into his boots for free, which was good because in reality the lads were flat broke.

Mike himself was newly married and nearly didn't go. As a general labourer on the docks, the '20-odd' pounds the trip cost was a lot of money. Mike and his wife Ann had just moved into their own house off Newbridge Road, but a sympathetic Ann wouldn't let him miss what she considered a once in a lifetime opportunity.

The boys were on such tight budgets that they ate chicken and chips for the whole trip, but Kay made sure that the women in their lives were not forgotten. She arranged for each player to take home a token gift, a small bottle of the Jacques Heim's perfume J'Aime, which inspired Christian Dior's own J'Adore. Heim, a contemporary of Dior, was a Parisian designer, manufacturer of women's furs and couture and the inventor of the bikini.

Luckily for me, Mike Bullock's wife Ann kept her bottle, and despite it being a little mouldy on the inside it still smells absolutely divine. Such a gift, however small, indicates that Kay thought holistically and realistically about the club. She understood that the women were making sacrifices at home so that their men could play international rugby league and deserved to be thanked accordingly. That she chose a Parisian designer's perfume showed that she thought they deserved more than a trinket, and that Ann Bullock has kept it these last fifty years shows how special the gesture was.

Kay made sure that for the team the France trip wasn't all about rugby league either. They received a cultural education visiting the Louvre and Notre Dame, and took in the sights, just as she organised.

The second match against Regiment de Jonville took

place on rock hard ground, in a big, but quite derelict stadium.

One Army player had a skinhead, which Mike said was odd and in Hull in 1963, rarely seen. When asked about it one of the French players managed to communicate the words 'bad lad' and explain that, in the French Army if you'd misbehaved you got your hair shaved off.

The semi-professionals won easily, but French officials praised East Hull's open style of play and numbed the pain of defeat for the visitors as they were treated to post-match champagne with the mayor of Paris, complete with some kind of 'posh biscuits' that Mike Bullock has still failed to identify but recalls looked like trifle sponges. The Mayor gave them speech in a French, and it rounded off their trip in style.

East Hull were defeated in France, but victorious at home, as that 1963/64 season also saw East Hull become the triumphant winners of the Council Cup.

Off the field, Kay's success and dedication to rugby league was such that in the same season she was the first woman ever to be appointed to the Hull and District Amateur Rugby League Council. The council's meetings of club secretaries took place at The Ritz club on Holderness Road on Tuesday evenings, where Kay would have been the only woman amongst approximately fifty men from the other teams in the leagues. 'At meetings I would imagine she gave as good as she took, knowing her!' smiled Mike Bullock.

However, despite her drive and spectacular achievements, in 1967 Kay disappears from rugby league history. We know from the Rugby Football League's Official Guides that Kay remained at the helm of East Hull until the 1966-67 season, when East Hull became New Embassy and Brian Robins took over as the new club's secretary.

'Happiness is an allegory, unhappiness a story'

IT would have been very easy to draw a line under Kay's story here, and put her achievements as rugby league's first known female coach and a highly successful secretary into the record book. But I couldn't draw the line, and I doubt I ever will.

For me, history is about human stories and all too often it is boiled down to the cold, hard facts of who did what and when, especially rugby league history whereby a reader is frequently given dry lists of player names, match scores and tables of points scorers. Given the obstacles many women have faced, and continue to face in the game, I feel that it is important to get a sense of who these women are and what drove them to push the gender boundaries and make in-roads into such a masculine sport.

Kay Ibbetson was not the first female amateur club secretary; that honour goes to Rosalie Kyle, who, in 1947 became secretary of Huyton Juniors for four seasons in the St Helens Junior Rugby League.

Kay was the next female secretary and clocked up six seasons at East Hull, and during her time only two other women took up posts in Keighley and Hensingham, each lasting one and two seasons respectively. What is remarkable about Kay in contrast to these other women, is just how dedicated she was and what she achieved beyond the secretarial role in her six seasons at East Hull.

And so I fell in love with Kay. Having spent months in the Rugby Football League archive looking for the proverbial needles in the haystack that are passing references to women, here at last was a woman who had really pushed the boundaries that society, and the culture of the sport, imposed on her gender. A woman who had made herself active in the masculine game she loved and even dared to enter the field and coach a team. Whilst the journalists were instantly smitten with her appearance - she was described tall, attractive and with extraordinary flame coloured hair - it was her achievements and tenacity that sprung out from the page and grabbed my heart.

Never before had I wanted to meet someone so badly. I felt sure that Kay Ibbetson would be more than the sum of her accomplishments in rugby league. I wanted to know more about her so I could attempt to do her story justice by putting her achievements into the full context of her life. So here is where I feel my real search for Kay began.

The only mention of Kay's family in any of the articles I'd read said that her love affair with rugby league began from an early age, when she used to slip under the turnstiles to watch Hull KR with her father. I could only hope that she had similarly passed on her love of the game to children or other relatives who were active in the game in some way. But how best to reach them?

Initially, I turned to the rugby league community for help. I put out a call for information via several online forums, and after several weeks I had one response from a gentleman in Queensland who played for East Hull in 1962, but more of that anon. Next, I printed over a thousand leaflets containing what information I had about Kay, plus a photograph, and handed them out around Craven Park before the Hull derby.

Wearing my usual black, the remnants of my Gothic teenage years, but sporting no Hull FC logo, it's fair to say I got an 'interesting' reception from some of the home fans and left wishing I too had developed 'cloth ears'. I took it as light-heartedly as I could, and every so often someone would say 'I remember her,' but further questioning showed that they knew she existed but never actually knew her, which is not surprising given that she had made the front page of the local paper.

A few helpful people took extra leaflets for friends they thought might know about her, and one man said: 'I remember her running a bus company, but that's all,' which gave me food for thought and a possible lead.

With not much new information to go on for my efforts, I turned my attention to tracking her down in a more traditional way. I mentally donned my deerstalker and set to work on telephone directories, electoral rolls and finding my way around several genealogy websites.

Time consuming database searches allowed me to piece together her family tree, and anyone who has tried this knows just how frustrating it can be for a beginner. The software is very unforgiving, and it was especially frustrating because when I finally found the entry for her birth I realised Kay had knocked five years off her age every time she spoke to the press.

It seemed that she was an only child, and I could find no death certificate, so with the hope that she was alive I traced her lineage back to both sets of grandparents, exploring the branches of aunts, uncles and cousins in order to see whether she had any living relatives. It's fair to say that I now know more about Kay's family than I do my own.

Kathleen Emily Ibbetson was born into a typical working-class family in the Sculcoates area of Hull on August 11, 1923. Her 27-year-old mother, Kate, came from Dundee and was the daughter of a shipyard driller.

Kate was the youngest of five children and had two

sisters and two brothers. By the time she was 14 the family had moved to Hull, no doubt due to her father finding work within Hull's extensive shipping industry. One sister was a domestic servant and the other a black lead worker at Reckitts, whilst her brothers were a shipyard labourer and a private in the army. A member of the 6th Battalion of the East Yorkshire Regiment, the latter died in 1915, aged 25, during the Gallipoli campaign.

Her father was born Thomas Ibbetson in Hull in 1894 and was the son of a general labourer and warehouseman.

In 1911, aged 17, Tom was a light porter at a paint factory alongside an elder brother. He had been born into a large family; his mother gave birth to twelve children in total between 1874 and 1894. The births and deaths of ten can be traced, and we know that Tom was one of only three brothers and seven sisters, but sadly only nine children survived in 1911.

Kate and Tom married in 1922 and Kay came along the following year. Kay was very close to her parents throughout their lives and in 1950, aged 27, she remained at the family's first known address, 8 Keble Grove, Preston Road, with her mother and father. How long they had been at the address prior to 1950 is not known, but they remained there until 1970 when 47 year old Kay and her mother moved to the recently-built Bransholme estate.

Kay set up her business, Clerical Services, which began operating from 25 Bishop Lane in the old town, in 1958. Clerical Services was an employment agency that also offered typewriting and copying services. Kay had a keen business acumen and according to *Rugby League Magazine*, business, rather than on the terraces at Craven Park, is where Kay 'developed the confidence and sure touch of mixing in a man's world'.

Telephone directories and electoral records allowed me to map her addresses through the city, and helped to uncover more information about her businesses. The electoral roll also revealed that she married at the age of 47, and that her husband disappeared quickly. With all sorts of questions going round in my head, I traced her through her married name, Maule, only to be utterly deflated when I found her date of death: March 20, 2005.

I would never get to meet this woman I'd begun to admire. I raced to the microfilms of the *Hull Daily Mail*, hoping to see several memorial notices that would lead me to those that knew her, but there were no messages of love from friends of family; all that appeared was a simple notification of death. With no mention of any family, and no other notices to go on, I had a horrible vision that Kay had died very much alone.

I set out to find her grave, hoping that it may give me some new information. At the crematorium I discovered where she was buried and so I set off for Eastern Cemetery, armed with three red and white roses, and found her unmarked grave.

I'm not ashamed to say that I cried.

I had become so wrapped up in Kay's story, that to see her grave with no headstone seemed like such an injustice. There lies a Hull woman, who made rugby league history, and no one would ever know. What made it more poignant is that the graves around hers were so flamboyant. I placed the flowers and felt that I owed it to her more than ever to find out more about who she was and celebrate her life accordingly.

Considering she had been so public in her rugby years, I could not understand why I couldn't reach anyone in the city who knew her. I looked back through the articles for names that might help, and realised that I may as well begin with Hull KR legend Alan Burwell.

I interviewed Alan, who began to add necessary detail to her time at East Hull, but as Kay was a very private person he did not really know her personally. However, he put me in touch with others and when the copy of her death certificate arrived, I found her next of kin, and friend, Julie. Slowly, I began to get closer to Kay.

I knew she was constantly registered as living with her parents throughout her life, and that such records seemed to indicate that Kay was their only child. However, Julie told me that Kay was not alone and instead had a younger brother, Michael. Michael was born in 1937 and was fourteen years her junior. How close they were as children is not known, and Michael is yet to be tracked down. I could only smile at the predictability of Julie saying that during her twenties Kay served abroad with the army.

We can begin to get a full picture of the woman Kay was from 1958, when she began her clerical agency and her pursuits in rugby league.

Mike Bullock remembers her as a happy, outgoing person who did all the organising for everything: 'She had a laugh and joke with you and you could say things back to her, she'd give you just as good like. That's the type of person she was. She was a character in her own right.' Mike can remember thinking:

> ...that she shouldn't come into the changing rooms when we were getting changed, which she did quite often. In them days it was quite embarrassing and we'd all turn around. It's not like now, nowadays they'll go in and do all sorts but in them days women didn't do such as that. But Kay was one on her own,

with her red flaming hair. Quite outward and boisterous was Kay; would put people in their place. Those are the things that you remember about her. She was well before her time, it didn't bother her at all. Kay socialised with everybody and took participation in most of the things. She did what club secretaries did and beyond that really.

My first respondent, Graham Rumble, who now lives in the Gold Coast area of Queensland, played for East Hull under-17s in 1962-63, and remembers that Kay 'was a very bubbly character and her enthusiasm rubbed off on the players. In our team were Ken Crane [brother of Mick] and Roger Booth, who signed for Hull FC.'

Graham recalls her being 'a very attractive lady with flame hair' and like Mike 'found it a bit strange when she was in the dressing rooms, but we got used to it after a while'. Generally, I found most players I spoke to did not know anything about her personally, but Graham remembers her being a fan of the American crooner Johnny Mathis and the boys teasing her about that. Kay left an impression, as he went on to say: 'For me to remember these things nearly fifty years on shows that she had an effect on us all.'

Kay's father Tom died in December 1967, his death coinciding with the time she left East Hull, however exactly why she left the club at the time of merger is not known.

In 1971, when Kay and her mum moved to Bransholme, her business, Clerical Services, ceased to appear in the telephone directory. Records for her company haven't been found, but it is perhaps telling that in 1962 when the category 'employment agencies' appears in the phone book Kay's was one of four listed. In its final year, it was one of seven, and in the following year there were nine competing for custom.

Perhaps a major factor in the closure of her business was her marriage in 1971 to Arthur Maule, who moved into Logan Close with Kay and her mother.

Arthur was five years younger than his bride (she was 47 at the time) and the former ship's cook from London already had one ex-wife to his name. What is curious about Arthur is that in 1948 he married his first wife, Joan, in Kensington, and they lived with Joan's parents in Camden for at least ten years. Here he was again, moving in with his wife's parents.

Together, Kay and Arthur pair set up K.E.A. Coaches in their name - quite literally, as it is possible the acronym stands for Kathleen Emily and Arthur. The new company were advertised as 'specialists in private hire at home and abroad' and operated out of Wincolmlee. However, the business did not last long, for in 1976, the adverts disappear, and a year later, so does Arthur's name from the electoral roll. On 17 June 1977, K&A International Hauliers file for bankruptcy, and the notice in the *London Gazette* lists Arthur as an HGV driver and Kay as a stenographer.

Marriage over, and seemingly in financial trouble, Kay then suffered what was perhaps her biggest trauma in 1979, when her mum, Kate, died aged 83.

She had lived with her mother for most, if not all, of her life. And the misery was prolonged as it took six years, until 1983, for the bankruptcy file to be closed, when Kay was aged 63. The following year, she moved into 88 Amberley Close, Bransholme, and in 1995 went round the corner to 105, the home that would be her last.

'Surely something resides in this heart that is not perishable'

IT was around the time of her final move that Julie met Kay, and the two became firm friends.

Kay was initially Julie's 'Avon lady' and from there she became her hairdresser. They became close, and Kay came to look upon Julie's family as her own and would spend hours talking to the family about coaching East Hull, her Challenge Cup experiences and players like Alan Burwell.

Herself devoted to East Hull, Kay disapproved of anyone not fully committing to the club. She told Julie of the time she berated a player who couldn't go to France simply because his girlfriend would not let him: 'If she'd committed herself to something, everybody should commit their selves to something and no amount of excuses would be tolerated; if she said she wanted him there [...] he should be there for the team and no mistaking.'

Julie remembered that Kay was proud of her time in rugby. She did meet obstructions, but: '...Kay never backed down. She was a feisty, determined person. And if she set her mind to do something she would see it through.'

Julie understands that in her post-rugby days, possibly in the 1970s, Kay worked as a steward on North Sea Ferries as a purser on perfume section: 'She's always worked in male society, like in the Army and on the ferries. So she sort of made her mark as a female working with men.'

Julie also remembers Kay as: '...a sweet old lady. Quite feisty; a typical redhead. Loved to be smart, prim and proper, always nicely turned out. She was always very slim and upright and did not leave the house without her make up on, face powder and lipstick, even at the end of her life.'

Kay remained independent until her final three years, getting out and about on her motorised scooter.

'She found her legs again and was never in,' said Julie. She was usually at bingo, or if she was at home, she would listen to BBC Radio Humberside or read. 'She would read anything and would never watch television before a certain time in the evening.'

An animal lover, Kay's best pal was a Yorkshire Terrier. She once broke her arm falling over it, but denied it was the dog's fault as she loved him so much.

Even in her latter years, Kay remained quite sporty and watched most sports, but rugby league was her passion. I am pleased that the sport never really left Kay's life, even though she left Hull's rugby league life behind.

She loved to watch games on television and never missed a match. She followed Julie's boys' amateur careers with interest and when the eldest signed for her beloved Hull Kingston Rovers was 'over the moon'. She would listen to both professional Hull teams on the radio, occasionally to Hull FC fan Julie's chagrin. Julie chuckled as she recalled: 'It used to be the first thing that greeted me on a Monday when I took her pension. "You did well again yesterday," she'd laugh, if we'd lost.'

Sadly, Kay's life after rugby was not easy. She told Julie of the pain of losing her parents.

'Her mum was her world,' Julie revealed. 'I think she suffered a breakdown when she died. She did miss her mum often. She'd spend hours talking about her mum, saying how she was a redhead and she'd inherited her temperament. She was "brought up proper" as she put it.' Sadly, Kay and her brother quarrelled and the relationship was never repaired.

As for Arthur, he remains something of a mystery and Julie doesn't know whether Kay ever divorced him.

'She was very private person, but I know she had a hard life. I think her husband wasn't the best of people for her. He dragged her down a bit. I never met him, but from what I heard when Kay spoke of him, I don't think there was any love lost when he went.'

Kay passed away, aged 82, from bronchial pneumonia and lymphedema. She was left a pauper and had just had enough money to bury herself. Problems with paperwork meant that Kay couldn't have a headstone or be buried with her mother, much to Julie's regret.

Having spent so long with Kay in my life, I was happy to hear that there had been about twenty people at her funeral. She didn't have many friends, but at least there were people there who cared about her at the end of her life.

Kay's autobiography is far from complete, but what we can say is that her achievements in rugby league were significant, as the first known female coach and a highly successful secretary.

These achievements were made possible by the quality of person Kay was, the influence of her mother's temperament, her desire to facilitate positivity in the lives of Hull's adolescents through youth club work and her early independence and motivation in business.

At the time she didn't get a sense of what she'd done in the game, and it wasn't until later in life that she realised she had broken new ground as a woman in a masculine sphere. She'd met with problems, but she never backed down; she'd never walked away from anything and she'd seen things through to the end.

I will always be sad that I never got the chance to meet this remarkable woman.

'If she'd have been in the suffragettes' times, Kay would have been one of the ones leading them,' said Julie.

13 Inspirations

'She was very strong-minded. She didn't think there were different rights and wrongs for both sexes.'

There is no doubt at all that Kay Ibbetson and I would have bonded over more than just our love of rugby league. Kay was a woman after my own heart, for whom if you did something, you did it as an individual regardless of your gender.

Who wouldn't want a woman like that at their dinner table?

● Victoria Dawson is a PhD candidate at De Montfort University and Heritage Manager at Rugby League Cares. If she could break the rules of the dinner game, she would also invite Marc Bolan.

13

8. Bradford's Gentle Giant

Brian Noble

WHEN the front door opened of our little terraced house in Yorkshire, it was as if someone had stolen the daylight. I was eight years old and terrified. I couldn't run because my dad was holding on to my lug-hole.

Filling the door was this huge frame of a bloke, this great big thing, just standing there.

I thought: 'This is it, my time is up.' I didn't know it at that moment, when my whirring, frightened brain could only think about escape; about how I might be able to duck and dart away from the monster on the threshold. But this overwhelming presence was going to be one of the most inspirational people in my life.

His influence would ensure that this snotty-nosed kid from a run-down area of Bradford would not go down the same nefarious and law-breaking path of his young mates. He would persuade me that going to school might not be a bad idea. He'd channel my energies into sport to keep me on the straight and narrow. And he'd introduce me to a strange new game I didn't really know too much about: rugby league.

His name was Trevor Foster.

This man's influence and inspirational approach had already cast its net far and wide. And so this is a story not just about his impact on myself, but also his influence on the game he loved and the city and community he adopted.

You'll read about:

- His extraordinarily brave decision to move up from South Wales in the 1930s, giving up his roots and daily contact with the family he loved
- His impact on rugby league as a princely second-row forward in one of the all-time great Bradford Northern sides
- His crucial role in bringing the city together to rescue Northern from extinction in the 1960s
- His role as an ambassador for the Bulls when the Super League era dawned
- And the selfless, unstinting charity work he quietly undertook around the city in which he lived, earning himself a Papal Medal, an MBE, but more importantly a place in the hearts of thousands and thousands of people

But as I say, I didn't know any of that back then. All I knew was that Trevor Foster was what they now call the Education Welfare Officer. In those days, he was the Board Man.

I lived in a place called Manningham - 232 Kensington Street, Manningham to be exact - a vibrant area for kids not going to school. The Board Man's job was to go round and grab you by your ear and drag you back to lessons.

That first meeting with Trevor, when my dad grabbed hold of me and hauled me, kicking and screaming to the front door to be 'introduced' to this fella, was only the first of many, many occasions when our paths crossed. He took me by surprise that day. After that I sometimes got lucky and when he arrived at the front door, I was out the back door quick before anyone could catch me. I'd either run to school myself or be off further afield and go missing for a couple of days.

But one time when I wasn't at school, he tracked me down, finally sat me down and spoke with me.

I can remember him saying how important school was, what an opportunity it presented. He clearly made an impression because I still remember a lot of his words about what was right and wrong and how upsetting it was for my mum and dad that I wasn't going to school. I only felt intimidated by his presence. His words were kind and supportive and forgiving. He was the amber flare I needed at that time of my life.

Trevor Foster was impressive. He had presence. He talked you through things and had a knack of grabbing you by the arm, making sure you were listening. There was no threat of violence but if Trevor spoke, you *were* listening.

He probably saw in me this little energetic, red-headed goofy kid with national health specs who needed an avenue. So he took me down to the Bradford police sports youth club, which was on Walker Drive in Manningham. He was a patron there and he had a huge influence on the place. He got me into lots of activities. They had a rifle range! Who would believe that? A rifle range with real guns!

There was also basketball, which was a new sport to us back then, so we played that too. Table tennis, boxing - he thought the odd bout in the ring might channel my energies and anger. And then some fight or other got called off and, as a 13-year-old, I started playing rugby league. Along with table tennis, it soon became a passion.

In those days, I didn't really associate Trevor with rugby league. I didn't know much about the game as we lived in the football area that Manningham had become since, despite being one of the founding members of the Northern Union and indeed the very first ever rugby league champions in 1895, its club had switched codes to the round ball game in 1903 and become Bradford City.

Until, that is, people began saying: 'You do know who that is, don't you?'

Then other kids would say: 'That's Trevor Foster.'

I had no idea he was famous, a legend in the city, but I did know he had a big booming Welsh voice and that when it went off you took notice. He had absolute respect from everyone. Was I scared of him? Yes, I think I was, but in the right way. He made me be a regular at school.

And he made me realise how enjoyable sport can be.

If there hadn't been a Trevor Foster around, I don't know how my life would have unfolded. I think 50 per cent of the kids from the area I grew up in turned to crime in one form or the other. A small proportion always fight their way out, but I'm pretty sure that, had I not been introduced to Trevor, I would have been in a little more bother than I was.

And it wasn't just me he was influencing. There were loads more like me. Trevor's son, Simon, has vivid memories of his father's role as a Board Man.

'I was a nipper when he started,' Simon says. 'And I remember him telling me the story of how he got his job as a welfare education officer because he was fairly fit and he was fairly big. He said: "I can run, chase 'em, grab 'em and bring them back to school." He was laughing, of course. But he was given the most disaffected areas of Bradford to work in.

'There were some hooligans there, lads who would take advantage. But my dad would bring them into line.

'I remember a boxing coach in Buttershaw, who also helped out at the police boys club. He was a PE teacher and said that every time Trevor was on his rounds, his colleagues knew everyone would be in school, on time, and stay there. It took a while for that to happen, though, about three terms. And it wasn't so much about discipline, it was that Trevor had a charm about him that would engage these lads. They would come back into school and they'd work pretty well.

'He took many youngsters down to the police boys club. When he retired at 65, they had a celebration farewell at the Town Hall and you couldn't get in because a lot of the kids he had dealt with down the years had found out he was leaving and wanted to be there.'

MY own professional rugby league career began when I signed for Bradford Northern, aged 16. I wasn't that good a player, but I was really hungry and Trevor was a hunger manager. He would make sure I did all the things I had to do to give myself a chance.

He was clever at football and would always be giving me tips, such as support this bloke there, or if you follow this bloke you'll get a few more off-loads and a few more carries.

But away from the field he taught me discipline. If there was bad weather or something and no buses, he'd say, 'well, walk.' That was five or six miles from where I lived, but I would walk it because of his influence. Even if it was snowed off, I'd got the determination to get there.

He gave you the feeling that problems were there to be solved, that nothing could get in your way.

Trevor was a gentle giant. His presence was not just about physical stature, he had an aura about him. Not many people have that. He sat there and you immediately thought: 'Respect'. He had a depth of knowledge and if you asked him an honest question he would give you an honest answer. He had integrity and was an absolute gentleman.

It was a relationship from that time of my life that I have not forgotten and I don't remember many others.

I don't think I have ever quite measured up to his standards, but that's how he inspired me. I aim to do so. Some people go under the radar, and at times he was a shy man. But when he said something, he meant it and we hung on his every word.

Whatever era of rugby he talked about, he was the most positive guy on the subject that I ever met. He loved Odsal with a passion and he would never bad-mouth the modern game. He would say this is a game that's as good as it's ever been and the athletes are too. Rugby league could not have had a better PR man, I don't think I ever heard Trevor say anything negative about anything. And if Trevor said it was good then it must have been, because he had seen and played with and against the very best.

'My dad transcended three eras of rugby league,' says Simon, his son. 'Briefly, there was the pre-Second World War when he turned professional in 1938, moving up north from Newport. Post-war, he was a key figure in the halcyon days of Bradford Northern and Great Britain. And then in the Super League era, he embraced the modern-day game with great enthusiasm, most notably as the Odsal timekeeper.

'That time shines through for me. I always remember his very first game, time-keeping. He spent most of the pre-match just walking around the stadium, enjoying time with the supporters, especially families. And once he got in the old covered stand, you just couldn't pull him away. When the time came to settle in at a quarter to three, he was lost in this great swell of atmosphere ... the flags, the singing. His enthusiasm for Super League made a big impression on me.'

Time for Trevor ran out in April 2005, when to widespread sadness in Bradford and across the game as a whole, he passed away following a short illness, aged 90, shortly after the publication of his biography. Simon, one of its trio of authors, worked out that 67 of those years had been spent at Bradford whether with Northern or the Bulls.

'In the Bradford Northern resurrection of 1963/64, when the club first got into serious financial difficulties, he became a true leader,' his son continues. 'As a father to me, that was no surprise. I had seen it very early in life when he was running the police boys club. He was a very fair man, the youngsters knew he was somebody very special, and that followed him throughout his life.

'My dad never drove a car. He passed the test, but he liked to walk. As a Board Man he would walk. If there wasn't a lift to get to training, he would go on foot. And in his latter days, even aged 88, sometimes people would pick him up en route from his home in Little Horton to Odsal and ask why. "This is the way I always get there," he'd say.'

Trevor was born in Newport in 1914, a difficult time at the start of World War One.

'As a grown-up, he used to kid people on he was two years younger than he was,' says Simon. 'In the hope, I think that he would get that extra contract before he retired. When the time came to leave South Wales, it was a very difficult decision for him to make. He was in the Welsh rugby union squad at the time, a reserve first forward in 1938, for a Wales versus Ireland match in Swansea. As it happened, he didn't get on that day, but he was only 22 and destined to step up. Lots of people at that time suggested he was going to be a big forward for Wales for many years to come.'

Two things, however, made up his mind.

'One was the economy down there,' says Simon, 'and the other was his sister. In the 1930s, life was a struggle. The family, in which there were six children, had a smallish pub bought by his dad, Richard, in a busy area near the docks in Newport. Then, one evening, Richard fell out of a tree while apple-picking and went blind, aged about 40. The youngest of the family, Trevor took it upon himself to look after his father. After school, for example, he would take him for walks and they'd have a great time together. So he was very reluctant to go north. He worried that his mum would be left with everything, even though the other brothers were there.

'The rugby league folk, though, kept chasing him. Wigan came down first and then Bradford. But Trevor also wanted to win another Welsh cap. The fellow from Bradford put £100 on the table and said: "Here you are. You can buy a Welsh cap with that." Trevor was unmoved. So £400 was put down, and still Trevor wasn't interested. At which point, his sister Freda came into the room and said: "What's this all about Trevor? Why don't you want to move north? You're being given a great opportunity. Dad can't keep this pub and keep us all going. It might be a chance for you to get a career. By the way, Newport play Cardiff this weekend. If you break your leg - you're out for six months."

'And that just turned him. He decided to go.'

Trevor's welcome in Bradford was terrific. 'It was like being back in South Wales for him,' says Simon. 'It had been a long trip and he'd never been much out of Newport before. But as a young man, the first player he met at Odsal was a chap called Bill Smith, a forceful prop. He had his arm in a sling and told Trevor: "I've broken this arm and I've also broken this and broken that. I don't know what the hell you've come up here for, you should have stayed with the soft game down south. You are going to get a beating here."

'It put Trevor off. Within 24 hours, he didn't know whether to stay or run away. But he was taken by the warmth and hospitality of the place and within a week or two he said he wanted to live in Bradford, get married in Bradford and work in Bradford for the rest of his life.'

Not surprisingly, for Simon Foster, despite all his father's on-field achievements, he recalls Trevor first and foremost as a family man who inspired him in many ways.

But there were, he says, three particular times when those inspirational qualities were spread far and wide, as evidenced in many of the obituaries written in 2005.

'One was the period of great Bradford Northern football which extended from the early 1940s,' he says. 'He captained Bradford when they played Wigan in the 1944 Challenge Cup final, over two legs. They then missed a year, but went to Wembley in 1947, 1948 and 1949. All the great stories I heard of his comradeship with the Welsh players,' Simon adds wistfully, 'the likes of Willie Davies, the great stand-off, Frank Whitcombe, the great character forward, and many others.'

The atmosphere at Odsal back then was created by general manager Harry Hornby and coach Dai Rees. There was a family spirit, they were all in it together and the supporters were included in that - with support of 30,000 to 40,000 people cramming in.

'Trevor was a leader during that time,' says his son. 'He shared the captaincy over his 17-year playing career with the likes of Ernest Ward. But he did captain them in big games, and he was seen as a leader on the field of play, with a very cool head. He inspired people not only with his class, athleticism and try-scoring - he was a very intelligent player on the field - but also his coolness under pressure. And never, during his whole career, was he cautioned by a referee. Very few have managed that. Although they were a great team, Bradford also set high standards.

'Once, he put his shoulder out in the first half of the game against Huddersfield,' Simon recalls being told. 'There were no substitutions back then, of course, but at half-time the doctor put his shoulder back, behind the stand, out of sight of the other players and supporters, and he went on playing. He was on the wing in the second half. For him, it meant nothing at all. He was just a warrior.

'My dad made over 400 appearances, and that is very special, especially for one club. He scored a lot of tries as well, over 120 as a second-rower. That was something special. It helped inspire people to watch and play for the club.'

Trevor retired from playing in 1955, by which time he was in his 40s. 'Though I actually saw him play in his 50s,' adds Simon. 'In a veterans game at Headingley in 1966, he scored a try, beating Joe Egan on the outside to score in the corner. He had tremendous physical and inner-strength.

'Then, after his playing days, he got into coaching. Not many people know this, but he was the first chief coach of the Rugby Football League in around 1949, followed by the great Leeds full-back, Bert Cook.'

The second era in which Trevor Foster's inspiration shone through was the 1960s during Bradford's decline into near obscurity. That, says Simon, was arguably his greatest achievement at Odsal.

'In 1963, when literally the club folded to nothing and went out of the rugby league, he decided, probably over a prayer at his local Catholic church, that someone needed to take hold of this and he would lead the renaissance of Bradford Northern. Typical Trevor, he did it in a quiet way, he was never a shouter. He led that 1963/64 reformation aided by Joe Phillips, the excellent New Zealand full-back, who became the chairman and it all came to a head at the famous St Georges Hall meeting, when they needed to raise £1,000 to have any hope of survival.

'I was probably 13 or 14 at the time, and he said to me before leaving: "Say a prayer, Simon, or this could be the end." I looked at him and he looked at me and the honest opinion was that it was do or die.'

St Georges Hall was the venue in Bradford where all the big musical acts had played, the only place that could take the numbers. 'And as my dad left the hall that night, the last one to leave, a little old lady, had waited outside with what was probably her pension and gave him £5. She said: "Trevor, I wanted to see you in person because I wanted to give you this. This is my money for this month. Please take it."

'That spurred him on, motivated him to organise more meetings and more public gatherings. And within a period of six months there were business people around him who were willing to help. Although when I say business people, I mean people who were maybe running a post office or a pub or a restaurant. Not big business. But eventually they were able to get the club back into the league.'

Trevor was very proud of that period, though not in any way demonstratively. It was just something happened.

'His best moment,' says Simon, 'came in 1964 - the first match after reformation against Hull KR and 13-14,000 came to see it. Northern were beaten, but no-one was ever happier than my dad that night. They were back on the straight and narrow and won the Yorkshire Cup a year later.

'My dad then got more involved behind the scenes and he was an interesting character in that way. I've thought more about it since he died, but he was always in the background. If something needed doing, he'd do it, unprompted, in a quiet, charming way in support of those in need - which is demonstrated by the great amount of charity work he did across Bradford.'

Trevor's first love, after his family, Church, the Bradford club and Odsal was helping people in need. In all, he served an amazing 50 years with the Bradford police boys club. 'He went twice a week and I always thought he was paid for going down there,' recalls his son. 'But I discovered when he retired that he wasn't. It was all voluntary. That's just the way he was. He went on to volunteer at Bradford Royal Infirmary, too, becoming a Friend of the Royal Infirmary and an ambassadorial figure there.'

After his father's death, Simon was given an invite to an occasion at the Infirmary at which they opened up the Trevor Foster Way, a circuit around the hospital for people to walk, especially those who have had a stroke or heart attack. His other two big charities were Cancer Research and the Bradford Hospices, which he helped for many years. He also did a lot of work for St Vincent de Paul - quietly in the background - which is a part of the Roman Catholic church.

'He was awarded a Papal Medal, a supreme accolade given by the Pope, for support for his community,' says Simon. 'That for him was worth more than his three Challenge Cup winning medals. He couldn't believe it. And of course he got his MBE for his work in the community too. A lot of people, even today, think he got the MBE for services to rugby league, but he didn't. He should have done. If anyone deserved that, it was him. But it was for the community work he did around Bradford.'

A man who had such an impact on so many people's lives also more than made his presence felt in the era of the Bulls. Along with being time-keeper, by now in his 80s, he became president of the supporters association and president of the past-players' association too. In fact, he started the players' association, one of the first people to form such an organisation and other clubs took a similar stance after that.

He was, says Simon, in his element at functions with the past players. 'You'd always wait for his five minutes of "bring on the revolution". He'd always gets quite animated and enthusiastic. He loved the game and he loved the people around it. When I was a youngster, I was taken to a lot of places with my dad. I'd go to the matches on the coach. I'd be pushed into the dressing room. I'd see his influence on the players, which was quite massive.

'Then, as I grew older, people would tell me what an inspirational player my dad had been. He never engaged me with tales of how he scored at Wembley twice, or how he became an influence and a leader on the Indomitables Tour of 1946, the first such trip in any sport after the Second World War. He stood above all the difficulties they had faced, the travelling by sea for a month and days on a railway train crossing the Nullarbor Plain. The fact that it was a frugal tour, with a lot of injuries including his own, didn't matter. He rallied the troops and even got involved with the Lions' traditional Welsh choir to raise a little more money for the far from well-paid players.

'And he was generally seen as a motivator. His fellow tourist, the Wigan hooker Joe Egan, always said that he kept morale high. But he never bragged to me about what he did; I've had to read all about it since and that humility was still there in the midst of Bullmania in the 1990s.'

Trevor was a figurehead in the early days of Super

League when, at what was now Bradford Bulls, we saw him as the most gentle, welcoming figure. He would welcome opposing officials - and players if necessary - to Odsal, always keen to look after their needs.

That was something which perhaps didn't come naturally to some of the directors, but Trevor saw it as his duty to make sure that people enjoyed the same warmth on arriving that he had first felt in 1938.

'He really embraced the Super League era,' says Simon, before bringing a blush to one old friend's face. 'It was inspirational to see how enthused he was by the whole thing. Bradford's great success in those days thrilled him. He said to me several times: "Brian Noble is the man to lead this club," - there was an affinity there going back to the boys club. And he was very pleased when that came to reality.

'As time-keeper, I could see the thrill in my dad's face when Robbie Paul was playing, particularly when Robbie scored that hat-trick at Wembley in 1996. The early Super League era was a very special part of his life and he enjoyed his rugby league as much as he ever had, even as a player. My dad's involvement was marvelous for us as a family.'

And to top it all, in 2003, then chairman Chris Caisley invited Trevor to lead out Bradford Bulls against Leeds Rhinos ahead of the Challenge Cup final at Cardiff's Millennium Stadium.

'From the letters I'd written as dad's secretary in later life, I was aware that he had a lot of ideas. And there were two things he was very keen on. He did a lot of work to try to get a rugby union versus rugby league match organised for charity, because he had played in such war-time games himself for good causes. Billed as Union versus League, they were played at Headingley and Odsal in the early 1940s.

'But he had also lobbied, while Wembley was out of

commission being rebuilt, to take the final to Cardiff. He wasn't alone in that, of course, but it came off. And so when he was asked to lead Bradford out, he was proud as punch; it was a very special day for him.'

Leading up to the game, he'd been down in South Wales for three or four nights, staying in the Angel Hotel.

He was around the town each night,' recalls Simon. 'He went into Newport to meet people who remembered him and had a fantastic few days. But it culminated in that big moment just before kick-off, with a certain Brian Noble, the head coach, just behind him. I talked to my dad afterwards, and he couldn't quite explain it. But for a moment there, as he walked out with the players and coach behind him, he took over as captain.

'He was in another bubble. It was as if he was back at Wembley with Bradford Northern. He took it upon himself to introduce each of the players down the line to the guest of honour, the Welsh Labour MP Neil Kinnock, when of course that was the head coach's job. Trevor should have stood still at the end of the line like a cavalry man. I could see it from the stands and turned to my wife and said: "My dad's taken over here."'

Don't worry, Simon. I completely understood.

After the game, a 22-20 victory for Bradford in front of 71,212 people, a delighted Trevor sat in the Angel Hotel with the players and the Cup, recalled some of the events from his own final appearances.

Says Simon: 'It was salutary for me that when he died, we had a very moving funeral at his Catholic church in Bradford and people who wouldn't normally go to church came on that day. I wasn't surprised it was full to over-flowing or that we had to open up an extra hall.

In there, too, were 60 of the youngsters he'd taken to

the Bradford police boys club, all of them now grown men who wanted to say their final goodbyes.

'The day before the funeral I'd got a little bit panicky when I realised we would need a public address system, so I went to the church to meet with the priest and there were people there already, looking to book their seats for the funeral. It was extraordinary.

'And then, a week or two later, when I went to collect my dad's ashes, I was in for another surprise. Normally in such circumstances, you are given a two-thirds-full flask to collect. I had two full flasks waiting for me.

'Trevor was big-boned, big-build and big-hearted.'

⬤ Brian Noble is a one-time coach of Great Britain, Wigan, Crusaders, Salford and Bradford, with whom he became the only man to coach a club to three Super League Grand Final victories (2001, 2003 and 2005). A formidable hooker in his playing days at Odsal, he captained the 1984 GB touring side to Australia and is nowadays a high-profile BBC pundit and regular guest on BBC Five Live's *Fighting Talk*.

9. Better Late Than Never

Phil Caplan

IT's a game that tells the story. A regular round match which, in the ultimate scheme of things, was not going to influence the outcome of silverware or have a blue riband attached.

What's more, it's a defeat, something that Jamie Peacock's radar hates to countenance. It comes mid-season 2014, at Wakefield, and Leeds have been beaten 16-14 after conceding a last minute try.

In a depleted pack which, including those on the bench, contains four teenagers, Peacock is, even more than usual, the man they look up to and sets the lead; something that is his raison d'etre.

The team make 410 tackles, he alone a tenth of them

and not a single one is entered in the missed column. Stirling enough for most.

But add to that 29 carries, the highest in the game and more than both the starting props pitted against him combined, and the gaining of 171 metres - only topped by his own full-back.

For good measure there are also three off-loads, not bettered in either colours and eight passes.

In a sport that breeds warriors, it is a seemingly superhuman, quality-infused effort and all the more remarkable for being unremarked upon.

It is an indicative measure of the supreme consistency that is taken as his given and, apart from those who play and coach with and against him, too often taken for granted.

There is one other figure that it is impossible to get away from and, being a televised game, will not fail to have been mentioned, indeed some fans have a twitter lottery to try and guess the time it will be revealed by the commentary team; he's 36.

Age and toll have wearied him but not outwardly. He is a Super League phenomenon, the only player with enough Grand Final rings to fit on all his fingers.

When Leeds won at Wembley later in 2014, his third success in the competition but first at the national stadium - the previous two coming against the Rhinos, for Bradford, in the capitals of Scotland and Wales - there wasn't a box left for him to tick, he had done it all.

But that's not why his story is so sensational; this is the ultimate *Boy's Own* tale.

Jamie Peacock was not marked out for greatness early, he didn't progress through the age groups picking up representative honours, there was absolutely nothing - even by his late teenage years when he worked as a roofer - that hinted he would go on to captain his country and be awarded the MBE, announced in the 2012 New Year Honours list, for services to the sport.

If his career had been in commerce he would be deemed the ultimate self-made man.

His autobiography is entitled *No White Flag*, the most apt description of him and chosen by his wife Faye.

Bramley-born, he was a late developer, following his mates to Stanningley where he was coached by his dad Darryl, whose work ethic as a self-employed denture-maker left a huge impression on his son.

Part of Jamie's incentive as he helped drive Leeds to an improbable defence of the Super League crown in 2012, the second time they had won it from the previously unconquered fifth spot, was for his dad, by then frail after being diagnosed with cancer.

'My dad is the hardest working bloke I know, for as long as I can remember and always made huge sacrifices; doing whatever it took to keep himself above the breadline and the family afloat,' Jamie said, when asked to choose his inspiration.

'There was never much money around and in the days when interest rates soared and nearly sent him over the edge, he was regularly putting in 16 or even 18 hour days - and still smiling. He knew it just had to be done and that set a terrific example.'

Tall and rangy as a junior player but, by his own admission, not blessed with natural ability, James - as he was originally known - made up for that with a desire to give his all for his mates, who he loved to socialise with afterwards.

Word reached the Bradford assistant coach at the time, Brian Noble, that Peacock might be worth looking at.

'I was one of the people involved who signed him as

head of junior recruitment under Matthew Elliott,' Noble recalls. 'He sent me up to Stanningley U18s one wet Sunday morning to watch this long, gangly kid who had slipped through the net.

'The rain was being blown in laterally, as it sometimes does up on Coal Hill, and I couldn't even be bothered getting out the car and sodden through to watch a kid who had missed the boat.

'Jamie might have been pretty uncoordinated but he must have run the ball in 50 times and made 150 tackles. He was blind as a bat too. From one kick off, he was stood on his own, apart from his team-mates and he went the other way to everyone else chasing the ball. It turned out he was following a white Morrisons carrier bag.'

For someone who has gone on to intimidate the world's best defences and grow increasingly statesmanlike on and now off the field as a media pundit with the BBC, the early days were wracked with self-doubt and introspection.

As Peacock told *Guardian* feature writer Donald McRae when his autobiography first came out: 'There are times, on the inside, when I feel exactly like that shy ten-year-old kid in those terrible NHS glasses. That part is the one you usually want to hide. But you've got to be honest. We're not all superheroes are we?'

Notoriously, on his way to trials at Bradford, he remained on the bus not believing himself to be good enough to join such company and returned home, his dad often making excuses for his non-appearances as the young James wrestled as to his worthiness.

Apart from trialing for the Leeds City Boys, he played no representative rugby and an incident with a firework that went through his foot aged 15 very nearly curtailed his career before it had begun. But then this was an infant who had nearly died after contracting a mystery virus and seemed to have a season ticket to the A & E department of the local infirmary as he grew up.

Contact lenses and a growth spurt at 17 saw his potential uncovered but, like so many who have hit the greatest heights in life, he is fuelled by overcoming adversity.

In 2003 he nearly severed and then lost his hand in a beer-fuelled argument but came back to be Man of Steel and, seven years later, getting towards the veteran stage, he suffered a knee injury that required a full reconstruction which not only ruled him out of Wembley but would have ended the career of a lesser man.

He returned the following season to help the Rhinos make history by becoming the first side to win the Grand Final from fifth spot, his contribution to the astounding feat, immense.

Stubbornness and an innate competitive streak, in part gained from his maternal grandfather who was a boxer and professional footballer, were evidenced in his earliest school reports and he also has two younger sisters who he looked out for in their formative years.

Such is his relentless nature that he can be seen out running on Christmas Day - without an iPod, naturally - believing that it will give him an advantage against his supine-for-the-day rivals.

He has regularly pointed out: 'I'm sure that my mental toughness, above everything else, has enabled me to get to the very top and helped to overcome my natural skill deficiencies.'

In the motivational speeches he now gives to high profile organisations such as KPMG and the NHS - and the England rugby union side - one of his key themes is that, 'there is very little traffic on the extra mile.'

13 Inspirations

NHS General Manager Claire Shepherd said of one of his presentations: 'Jamie was truly inspirational and *No White Flag* impacted on us as a team as we attempted to plan and problem solve our own dynamics, and how we needed to engage and get the best out of our wider teams for the future.'

As he began to conquer his inferiority complex, he could have signed initially with Wakefield but they failed to come up with a viable offer and, aged 19, in 1997 he was inducted into a hierarchical Bradford dressing room that contained the likes of influential mentors Bernard Dwyer, Brian McDermott, James Lowes and Graeme Bradley.

Also in the Bulls' junior ranks but very much ahead of him in the pecking order initially was Stuart Fielden, already almost the finished raw-boned athlete, and a training target for the aspiring Peacock.

It took him two more years to break into the first team and even then head coach Matt Elliott had doubts he would make it, both physically and because of his withdrawn nature. It needed all Brian Noble's powers of persuasion and a word from Peacock's dad to a scout at Odsal to keep him doggedly on the path.

'He deserves all the plaudits himself, his growth and development as a rugby league player should be used for youngsters as an example of perseverance, resilience and not giving in because there were plenty of times he could have,' Noble says. 'We sent him to Australia, to Illawarra, to gain experience and he supplemented his wage working on the doors there. When he came back, he still couldn't get a shot and was loaned to Featherstone.

'His story is magnificent. He was 21 before he broke through and when the penny dropped for him, his desire to be a professional player was astonishing. He made himself the first name picked on the sheet.'

When at Wollongong University, he came under the tough love of feisty former Hull and Warrington half-back Greg Mackey, another vital part of his necessary learning curve about what it took to become a career rugby player.

When Mackey passed away from cancer scandalously young in September 2014, Peacock said: 'He had a massive impact on my early career. I wouldn't have made it as a pro without his input.'

Back at the Bulls and no longer on the outer, Matthew Elliott was another who gave the by now rampaging second-rower a reason to achieve.

The bluff Aussie was short on communication skills to those on the fringe and, despite him being a regular off the bench in 1999 and turning matches, left Peacock out of the Grand Final squad at the culmination of that year.

It was a key moment. Peacock vowed: 'It put fire in my belly to train so hard and play so intensely that should the same option ever arise for a coach, he would have no choice but to pick me; it forced me to raise my own personal bar rather than drink it,' retrospectively acknowledging that Elliott was probably right to omit him as he wasn't ready for such a stage.

Within a year he had won his first medal, under Elliott, playing in the Challenge Cup final and debuting for England in the World Cup and, the following season, as his star rose, scored on his Great Britain Ashes debut with his first touch.

Brian McDermott, as complex a character as the sport has fostered, is ideally placed to evaluate Peacock's transformation from reticent to resplendent.

Another who came to rugby league late and went from perceived jobbing prop to an international with unstinting effort as opposed to deft skills being his stock in trade, straight-talking ex-Marine McDermott pulled no punches, especially when it came to giving the emerging strutting Peacock advice.

He took over as head coach at Leeds in October 2010, with Peacock among his chief of staff.

Such is the respect McDermott holds for his protégé that, when Peacock launched his autobiography in Leeds, the then London Broncos coach came up especially for the day, unannounced, just to lend support and pay tribute.

'He gets energy when he's tired from somewhere. I'm such a lucky bloke to be coaching him, he's one of the modern day greats, he just continually bangs out top-end performances week-in, week-out,' McDermott says of his lead storm trooper.

'If you want to talk about stats, he wins the metres battles and he is invariably in the top two or three tacklers, with least misses; his poor games are still very, very good.

'It comes down to how Jamie Peacock conducts his life and what he does away from the club. His favourite saying is the extra mile is a lonely road. That's usually when you are away from the club.'

Not only is there obvious mutual admiration, the pair often seen deep in conversation after matches, and a shared front-rowers bond about what the role constitutes and the sacrifices needed to stay at such a high standard for so long, but they are absolutely at one that it is, first and foremost, about the team; the inner sanctum.

'As you get older, it's a bit of a cliché, your mind starts to think but your body can't keep up,' McDermott has stated. 'In JP's case it can. He's physically able to do what his mind has learned. Sometimes in the dressing rooms he doesn't need to be that articulate, he just tells you what to do.

'Every coach would like two or three people that can

just give a poke and a prod, they carry those messages through far better than any coach could. He's certainly one of those.

'His standing in the sport, his age, the influence he has over individual games. It's not a symbolic gesture having him in there, he's a very important player.

'Then you start taking into account what he's already won and you wonder where his drive continues to come from. He'd be on his own, one in a million. I don't think we'll get another one like him.'

As a young buck alongside, the pair often speaking of 'the trenches', McDermott spotted the qualities that have become the Peacock stamp.

'He was equally determined back then. He wanted to run through brick walls but kept running through the wrong ones. It's been a privilege to be involved with him, to watch him come through and develop from a big silly lad into a big wise one.'

His last game at Bradford was the exact opposite of McDermott's, who had been in the Bulls side that controversially lost the Grand Final to St Helens in 2002, and it has always rankled with Peacock that his chief adviser did not go out with the winner's ring he felt he deserved.

Peacock, though, despite being in incredible pain from a fearsome, accidental blow to his most sensitive area, had a fairy tale finish to his career at Odsal.

Skipper by then, and it having been announced that he was moving to greatest rivals Leeds, his boyhood supporting club, steered Bradford on a 12-match unbeaten run, taking them from no-hopers to trophy lifters from third spot, the first time it had been achieved from outside the top two.

Having taken some flak from the Bulls fans when the

impending move was announced on 1 September, six weeks later he made sure his future employers were downed at Old Trafford to seal the best possible send-off.

As so often, it was a performance that silenced the doubters.

His transition into the Rhinos' blue and amber he coveted in 2006 was more difficult than he imagined, a rare fallow year in ones where he has been an almost automatic Super League Dream Team selection, his 2014 shirt in the composite best of season side, nominated by journalists, a record breaking tenth.

He arrived at Headingley Carnegie as Great Britain skipper and having given first glimpses that his future lay as an unrelenting front-rower, but tried too hard to create an impression, his performances, by his own admission, petering out towards the end of the campaign.

There was also the strange scenario, to the outside world at least, that although he led the national side, the armband was firmly held by Kevin Sinfield at Leeds.

The coach who recruited him home, Tony Smith, reckons that the manner in which Peacock readily agreed to put the team above self, regardless of stature, is another measure of the man.

'You can't know exactly what you're getting when you sign a player, but I knew that it was going to be good in terms of the package he brought,' Smith recollects.

'I'd admired Jamie on the field and knew him reasonably well, but until you're in there fighting together, that's when you learn the most about each other.

'He came from a different culture and it was a little bit difficult for him initially, he had to make some adjustments and we adapted to what he brought to us.

'It was nothing but a pleasure working with Jamie.

He was one of those ultimate warriors that you come across in rugby league; he plays hard, tough and fair and you don't want much more.'

Of the captaincy issue Smith continues: 'It could have been difficult for him - and, at times, it probably was - he'd been very vocal and a big leader within the Bradford group. We'd already got a number of good leaders on and off the field so he needed to tone some of that down slightly in that respect and he did it very, very well.

'We sat down and talked about how it would work and it showed me that it wasn't about him. JP was very much a captain within the group and still is.'

Smith, when taking over the national reins towards the end of 2007, had no hesitation in retaining Peacock as skipper of his country.

'You need a lot of leaders, whether the "c" is next to their name or not; he's a leader and the other players look to him and listen to him. He hasn't got the ego that he insisted on being named the captain so that people on the outside know his worth to the group. Just by doing the role is enough for him.'

Like so often, though, those club setbacks of 2006 - inglorious defeat on his former stamping ground against Huddersfield in the Challenge Cup semi-final being, by self-admission, one of his worst-ever performances - super-charged him and he became the greatest transfer in Super League history.

The pent-up frustrations of that domestic campaign saw him take out his angst on the foe he most enjoyed beating, the Aussies, crystalised in, arguably, his finest display; Great Britain's Four Nations win in Sydney.

Coming off a narrow but unlucky defeat against New Zealand, the Lions were understandably seen as no-hopers facing the Green and Golds, only 25,000 turning up to witness an apparent foregone conclusion. The skipper, as was his trademark calling card, however, had other ideas.

Leading in the only way he can, by voracious deed, he set the template.

His try just after half-time to establish a 12-6 lead, where he dragged half the Kangaroo pack over with him, was the catalyst for GB's first defeat of Australia on their soil for 14 years. But it was for an incident in the third minute that the game is best remembered for.

Willie Mason, never the shy, retiring, wallflower type, decided he was going to be a human wrecking-ball, dispatching Stuart Fielden with a punch that broke his nose and disposing of Sean Long as if he were a rag doll.

In strode Peacock, the colossus. With a beautifully timed straight jab to the jaw, he put Mason on the floor.

It was a throwback to what had been a mainstay of clashes between the nations. But it made a huge statement to his own team as much as the opposition, that the skipper was not going to allow his team to be intimidated, he would stand full-square up for them; it was the archetypal refusal to take a backward step.

Such macho displays won the utmost respect from his international peers and further established a growing worldwide standing that saw him selected in the World XIII from 2005-07 and as International Forward of the Year that season and the one after.

In a column as a pundit for the BBC prior to the 2013 World Cup, when he was an enlightening part of their much-vaunted coverage, Peacock stated: 'Back in 2002, I was a member of the Great Britain side humiliated 64-10 by Australia in Sydney. 'It was a one-off Test and the preparation was terrible. Back then, I was young and naive. When I woke up the following day and saw headlines that talked about the "death of rugby league", I thought I had contributed to that process.

'But if that was an incredible low, then my high point as an international player also came against Australia.

'I was captain of the GB team ... in 2006. Towards the end, I was exhausted and miles behind play as we broke away to score the decisive try through Gareth Raynor.

'It was a cinematic moment as I watched the move unfold in front of me. All of our boys jumped up in realisation of victory as, simultaneously, the Aussie heads fell. The only rugby league shirt that hangs in my house is the one I wore that night.'

The following season, Jamie Peacock led the Lions to a home whitewash against New Zealand.

What mattered most for such a fiercely proud patriot, brought up on how much the red, white and blue shirt resonated, was that it was retired in style, central funding changes seeing the reversion to individual nations.

His international retirement came in mid-2012 following the accolade of the 2000-2010 British International Player of the Decade and, his proudest moment, when he was awarded the MBE by the Queen, unthinkable even ten years before.

The decision to give up the national shirt was the hardest of his career.

'To play for and captain your country is the highest honour and this was a decision that was not taken lightly,' Peacock said at the announcement. 'I felt that the time was right for me to step down and solely concentrate on playing for my club.

'In 2000, when I made my debut, it was beyond my wildest ambition and dreams that I would then go on to represent my country nearly 50 times and captain them for seven years. Against the best in the world I have always enjoyed rising to the challenge and played with passion, commitment and honesty.'

His chief executive at the Rhinos, and one time GB Assistant Coach, Gary Hetherington added: 'Jamie has given every ounce of blood, sweat and tears to the national set-up and it will be a massive challenge to replace such a fantastic athlete and captain.

'He is the perfect role model for any aspiring junior wanting to be the best they can be. The way he inspires those around him is his distinct quality. He epitomises everything you'd want from an international player. He's proud, he's patriotic and he's a very determined character. He's won the admiration of the Australians and that is not an easy thing to do.'

Peacock's form was such at the end of that season that many wondered if the decision was premature, club coach Brian McDermott saying, as Leeds somehow retained the title from fifth spot: 'JP's a freak and he's been doing that for a number of weeks now. He's sensational and has showed in these games just what toughness is.'

But, in character, there was no reconsideration, despite the prospect of righting a World Cup wrong, England short-changing in Australia in 2008.

'I asked Faye if she would mind if I competed,' Peacock said. 'I also had discussions with England coach Steve McNamara as well as my Leeds team-mate - and England captain - Kevin Sinfield. However, in the final weeks of the Super League season, it was obvious my busted, 35-year-old body would not be able to rise again. It might have been different if my dad was still here and wanted me to pull on the shirt one last time.'

Darryl lost his long, hard-fought battle the morning after Leeds had won, against the odds, at Wigan in early September 2012.

'It is a mark of the man and his dedication and commitment to our club that he played on Thursday night,' said McDermott when the news emerged. 'Not only did he play, just as his dad would have wanted him to, but he was once again one of our leading players in the victory.'

Such is Peacock's single-mindedness that he has even plotted his club retirement, pin-pointing the close of the 2015 campaign as the cut-off date.

When the time comes, he will be judged as a cornerstone and kingpin of one of the greatest eras in Leeds' history.

He was an integral part of their historic 'three-peat' when becoming the first side to win a trio of consecutive titles, from 2007-09, playing in all but 17 minutes out of the 240 possible at Old Trafford in the deciders.

Rhinos Player of the Year in 2008, 2013 and 2014, he has matured like a vintage port.

After a game at Castleford early in 2014, Brian McDermott said: 'I tried to take JP off three times but he just turned round and said "no". I need help.

'Does anybody dare tell JP to come off?'

And, after Peacock had played his 500th career game at Wakefield, McDermott added: 'I don't think there's been a more important or iconic player in Super League.

'To have been a big player on such a big stage, so consistently and over such a period of time he'd have to be the best.

'Never mind he is the most successful player in the history of the competition, to come up with the type of figures that he is still doing is remarkable.'

That season's glory was the missing piece of his and the side's jigsaw, the Challenge Cup win at Wembley.

Tellingly, afterwards, the players would not countenance talk of 'relief' and Peacock - having just made his 250th appearance for Leeds - was at his most unequivocal. 'It's euphoria,' he stated categorically. 'That should be the over-riding emotion.'

For the second successive year he was shortlisted for the Man of Steel and was awarded the Rugby League Writers and Broadcasters' Player of the Year prize, renamed after doyen Ray Fletcher for the first time; the type of player whom the *Yorkshire Post*, *Rothmans* and statistics guru would have unquestionably approved.

Paul Anderson, the Huddersfield coach and a former Bradford team-mate with him in the Bulls' engine room noted: 'He's had that level of commitment throughout his career. From a slow build-up he's gone the long way round to be where he is and that's a credit to him and his family and those around him for the longevity he's showed.

'He's a great player, a great bloke and a good ambassador for the game. He says the right things and the truth.'

Jamie Jones-Buchanan was with Peacock at Stanningley and has stood full square alongside him during the Rhinos years, the pair both now putting so much back into their local community.

Peacock even referees the Stanningley U7s on a Sunday morning, his son Louis tiptoeing into his footsteps.

'He's a leader, he always has been,' Jones-Buchanan says of his close friend. 'He's had a real influential and inspirational effect on my career. He's a Bramley lad, grown up in the same places I did, played for the same amateur club, both not very good looking, so we've got a lot in common.

'But one of the things he has that not many people do is that strength and ability to go through any pain barrier to get the job done, no matter what.

'It's a quality that is stronger in him than anyone else I know. He's world class week in, week out without any let up. He's an amazing character.'

Brian Noble, who played a key role in starting Peacock on the road to domination and appointed him both club and international captain, has absolutely no doubt as to what underpins the man.

'I have nothing but admiration for him, he is an astounding fellow and has had some life experiences,' Noble further elaborates. 'He has become a great leader. He doesn't push on every play but he used to say to me: "Don't ever take me off."

'Sometimes he looks like his whole world had fallen apart and every entrail is hanging out his backside but then, all of a sudden, he comes up with a game-breaking, world class, unbelievable play. He knows how to manage his energy and is always involved in the game, emotionally as well as physically.'

Noble continues: 'The respect he is held with among his peers is clearly there to be seen and on the international front he has been a top class performer for over ten years. Bearing in mind he came to the game late - and in the position he plays - how good is that?

'His skill levels have improved as he worked at his game with meticulous preparation but, what I can't stress enough is his total, focussed determination to be a professional rugby player.

'It is a salutary lesson that, whatever obstacles are put in your way, you can get either over or through them as Jamie did.'

Rugby league has given Jamie Peacock an all-round education in its widest sense and not just that, through it, he is currently completing a Masters' degree in Sports Business Administration.

The game has transformed him, along with becoming a family man, and made him a far more complex character.

If he does take up a role within the governance of the sport, heaven help those who don't like to hear the situation told as it is.

As he said leading in to the 2008 World Cup: 'It's unbelievable to think that 13 years ago I was that shy kid lifting tiles on a roof. I don't think any other international captain, in any sport, can make that claim.'

● Chronic lack of talent, stature and determination prevented Phil Caplan from playing rugby league. Managing editor of *Forty-20*, keen expansionist and trustee of the Leeds Rugby Foundation; the long-time writer and broadcaster collaborated with JP on *No White Flag* and is a big fan of cake.

10. A Call to Arms

Andy Wilson

NOEL 'NED' KELLY was, as his nickname suggests, a tough player. A very good player - he was named hooker in Australian rugby league's Team of the 20th Century, which puts him above some outstanding ones. But bloody tough. Any book about Hard Men, or the Era of the Biff, and he'd be in it.

Anyway, he'll never forget the first Test Match he witnessed in person, at the Brisbane Exhibition Ground on July 5, 1958, because of an exhibition of courage of which even he remains in awe. 'I wouldn't have been very old [he was 22, and yet to make his senior rugby league debut], and we went across from Ipswich,' Kelly recalls. 'I think I was a butcher then, working at a place called Redbank.'

The Exhibition Ground, also known in Brisbane as the Showgrounds or the Ekka, is now a heritage-listed venue, having hosted a wide range of significant events, from the first overseas visit of Queen Elizabeth II and the Duke of Edinburgh in 1954, not long after her coronation, to Don Bradman's Test match cricket debut against England in 1929.

It had a considerable league history, too, having been the stage for Great Britain's series-clinching victory in the first Ashes series in 1910 - Jim Leytham scoring four tries in a 22-17 win for Jim Lomas's tourists - and numerous State and club fixtures. But for Noel Kelly among many others, it will always be remembered as the venue for the Battle of Brisbane - and the heroism/masochism of Alan Prescott, the St Helens and Great Britain captain.

'It was very silly of me really,' recalled Prescott, in surely one of the most self-deprecating understatements in sporting history. Very silly? Prescott, a flame-haired wing-turned-prop who had just turned 31, and was captaining a Lions team who had lost the first Test of the series in Sydney, broke an arm in the third minute. Nothing but a flesh wound, he growled, decades before the *Monty Python and The Holy Grail* team dreamed up John Cleese's limbless Black Knight.

Exactly two weeks later, Prescott was being carried around the Sydney Cricket Ground - with his plastered right arm in a sling - by his fellow Lions who, perhaps inspired by his silliness, had retained the Ashes with a 40-17 win.

THE early years of Alan Prescott's distinguished rugby league career were unremarkable enough. The fact that he started out as a wing, with the Widnes St Maries amateur club from whom he was signed by Halifax, is certainly unusual, given the immortality he was to earn as a prop - although former team-mates such as Ray French and Alex Murphy argue that it was his pace, as much as his courage, that made him such a special forward.

It was after St Helens signed him for a £2,275 transfer fee in January 1949, for a debut against Belle Vue Rangers, that he was persuaded to switch to the front-row. Jim Sullivan, the Welshman more closely associated with Wigan, has been credited with that decision, but it would appear to have been down to his predecessor as Saints coach, Peter Lyons.

The move went well enough for Prescott to play for England against Wales and France in 1950, and to win his first Great Britain cap in November 1951, in a series-clinching 20-19 win against New Zealand at Swinton. He went on to wear the blue and red Vee on 28 occasions, the last of them at the Brisbane Exhibition Grounds in 1958, in addition to playing 11 times for England.

Success with Saints was not a given, however. The 1930s and '40s had been mostly lean, with the rugby team's struggles reflecting a town that was hit hard by the national Depression. They finished 20th in the 31-team Northern Rugby Football League season of 1951-2. Prescott's Saints years were not consistently glittering. But the appointment of Sullivan in 1952 led to a change of fortunes.

In the 1952-3 season, Saints finished top of the table and won the Championship, beating Halifax in the final, and also reached their fourth Challenge Cup final - the club's second Wembley appearance - in which they were strong favourites, only to be stunned by two tries for the Huddersfield teenager Peter Ramsden.

The following season, when Brian Bevan was in his pomp for Warrington and a fair few went to watch Wire's Challenge Cup final replay against Halifax at Odsal, they beat Wigan to win the Lancashire Cup. But it was in 1955-56 that Prescott achieved St Helens immortality, without breaking any of his limbs, by scoring a try, making another, winning the Lance Todd and becoming the first Saints captain to lift the Challenge Cup, after their 13-2 victory against Halifax.

'I was still playing union then, and I went down to London with three mates on the train,' recalled French. 'We did the usual things, Leicester Square, Piccadilly Circus, and then went to the match. Prescott had a very good game. Don't forget it was against Halifax, who had top class props, and were renowned as one of the best sixes in the game at the time. He did lead the way. I can picture him now, he used to really charge down the middle at a fierce pace, and of course he had red hair. He was quite a ferocious sight striding down the middle. With the pace he had having started his career on the wing, he'd have been an ideal prop today.'

A few months later, Prescott, the first forward to captain the national team, led from the front throughout the Ashes series which Great Britain sealed by winning a third Test decider at Swinton 19-0, with Billy Boston scoring one of their five tries. Saints remained competitive, without winning any more trophies, for the next couple of seasons, and Prescott remained the national captain at the age of 30 when the Lions arrived in Wollongong for the first game of the 1958 tour.

Prescott's party included five other Saints, one of them an 18-year-old scrum-half who had only been a first-team regular for that 57-58 season. 'Alan was my saviour,' insists Alex Murphy, still with audible emotion in his voice even though he has discussed Prescott on so many occasions since his mentor's death in 1998.

'As a kid in my first game it was him who got me through it, told me what to expect, not to worry about mistakes too much, just sort it out on Tuesday. Then when I'd been picked for the tour, we had a game against Wigan and I had a bit of a problem with Mick Sullivan, but Alan told me what I'd done wasn't acceptable, and that I had to rise above it. When we went to Australia it was exactly the same.'

What a tour it was. From Wollongong they went to Orange, then to Newcastle, and even before the first Test they had beaten a Sydney selection including Jack Gibson and a young Johnny Raper in front of a near-50,000 crowd, followed by a brutal encounter with New South Wales. But the Test did not go well, with the Lions 18-0 down at half-time, eventually losing 25-8 as even the mouthy Murphy suffered stagefright.

'We lost the first Test through bad selection and that had to be sorted out before we played the second Test,' Prescott told French for a chapter in his invaluable book, *The Match of My Life*. 'There was a lobby to drop Murphy, but both Tom Mitchell [the tour manager] and I knew what he could do against Keith Holman [Australia's wily half-back] and we fought to keep him in the side. We knew we had to win this Test or we would be flying home as failures.

'To lift everyone's spirits, we moved to Surfers Paradise to do our training and we even, for the first time ever on a tour, trained at Surfers on the beach. The Aussie press laughed at us because the holiday resort is well-known for bikini-clad girls, gambling, nightclubs and every distraction you can think of for fit, young men. But the lads buckled down to training. It proved the ideal preparation, and we were ready for anything.'

Anything? In the third minute, Prescott went to tackle Rex 'Moose' Mossop, the 30-year-old ex-union international who had made his league debut for Australia in the first Test, and was to show heroism himself by playing in the 1959 Grand Final with a suspected broken jaw - before using that jaw to such entertaining effect as a television commentator.

'I knew it was broken,' Prescott recalled. 'I tackled Rex, my arm struck his head and smashed, and as I raced to get up the arm was numb and just buckled under me. I had heard and felt the crack. It was very painful but I carried on for a while until I went off to get our coach, Jim Brough, to put tape around the arm and strap it up. I don't think Jim realised it was broken.'

Speaking to the Saints Heritage Society, Prescott revealed that his club coach, the great Sullivan, was also an inspiration. 'Jim's words came back to me - "If you are only on the field in the way, then someone has to beat you. Always stand and face the opposition, never turn your back." It was very silly of me really because there could have been so much damage. But in my opinion I just had to battle on, especially when David Bolton left and we were down to 12 men. If I had called it a day then, that would have been the end of us.'

Bolton, the Wigan stand-off who would join Balmain and settle in Australia, had to go off with a broken collarbone in the 17th minute. Warrington wing Jim Challinor and another Saints legend, Vince Karalius, were also struggling with respective shoulder and back problems which required hospital treatment after the match. As French notes with splendid understatement: 'It was a difficult time, to say the least.' But Prescott and his team had been heartened by the start they made to the game, injuries notwithstanding. In the fourth minute, immediately after the captain's blow, Murphy made a blistering break and combined with Eric Ashton to lay on the opening score for Challinor.

'Jim Challinor's try at the corner did more for us to win this match than anything,' Prescott recalled. 'It came at just the right time, and gave us all heart.'

By half-time they led 10-2, Murphy having also played the key role in a second try, for Mick Sullivan, with Eric Fraser kicking two goals. But surely, they would have to cope for the rest of the game without their captain.

'I'd seen him do it, and the fact that he stayed down

showed how much pain he was in,' said Murphy. 'He was one tough man. But I don't think he let on to the physio. He got up, went to the next scrum - in those days they were proper scrums, you had to push in the front-row - and somehow carried on. I could not believe that any man could go through that much pain, and still be on the field. Then we went in at half-time and saw the state of his arm. But he got up off the bench, gave the team talk, and said to the doctor: "By the way, I'm going back." The doctor called him a Pommie maniac. Then to the rest of us, Alan said: "Let's go out and do it."'

Thanks to French, we also have Prescott's own account. 'The Australian doctor took a look at my arm and told me I must come off. But I looked around the dressing room and knew that the lads wanted me to stay on. They weren't aware it was fully broken. Spirits were high despite our problems, and I knew the loss of another player could send those spirits low. I had to stay on; there was no way I was leaving the match. The Aussie doctor washed his hands of me, and Tom Mitchell said it was my decision. I thought to myself "I can be of nuisance value - the Aussies will have to run round me."'

He did much more than that, as Mitchell recorded. 'He gathered the ball, he ran, he dictated the pattern of play and he tackled well with his good arm. Only those present at the game had any idea of the man's naked courage.' Nobody mentioned litigation, or health and safety.

No-one was more inspired than Murphy. Early in the second half he burst clear again to set up a third try, this time for Ike Southward, and again goaled by Fraser. 15-2. But the Aussies stormed back with three tries, only one of them converted, and although Southward scored a second for the Lions, Prescott felt a 20-13 lead was precarious with ten minutes remaining, as they packed down for a crucial scrum near their own line. 'I knew we must win the ball at this scrum,' said Prescott. 'If we didn't, I sensed we'd go under.' He thanked another famous ex-Saint for ensuring they did, even though in the process he suffered more excruciating pain.

I've always bracketed Dick Huddart with Karalius, as the most exotic-sounding back-row combination I never saw. Karalius, the formidable Widnesian who had been given one of the best nicknames in the history of all sports by Australian crowds - the Wild Bull of the Pampas - had taken over from Bolton at stand-off in this match, and recreated some Knowsley Road training ground routines with Murphy.

Huddart was a famously tough Cumbrian, the sort who made the bravest Lancastrians and Yorkshiremen wary when they travelled to the far north-west. He only joined Saints, from Whitehaven, after the 1958 tour.

'As we packed down for the scrum I shouted to the lads, and especially to Dick, who was in the second-row behind me, that we must have a huge push, that we desperately needed the ball,' Prescott recalled. 'Suddenly Dick rammed himself into the scrum behind me like a raging bull. He was all fired up, and he swung his arm around to bind me into the pack. But he grabbed the wrist of my broken right arm. I thought he had pulled my hand off the arm. I have never known pain like it in my life, it was unbelievable. I screamed, catapulted forward, and pushed like I have never done in my life. We won the scrum, kept the ball, and [after Holman and Karalius exchanged late tries] won the match.'

Murphy recounts that the dressing room afterwards was a strange combination of exhilaration, exhaustion and medication. With the series level, Prescott and several others headed for hospital. 'The lads went round to see Alan, and the first thing two of them did was dive on the bed,' says Murphy. 'For once it wasn't me being naughty. I was still in awe of what he'd done, and concerned about the damage.'

The fit players headed for Toowoomba, then Lismore, where Ashton took over the captaincy and scored four tries and seven goals in a 56-15 romp against NSW North Coast.

Then it was back to the Sydney Cricket Ground for the decider, watched by a 68,720 crowd including Prescott, with his right arm in plaster. With Barrow's Phil Jackson as stand-off and captain, Mick Sullivan scoring a hat-trick, and Karalius and Murphy again outstanding, the Lions won the series with plenty to spare, 40-17 - and summoned their injured captain to take the trophy on a lap of honour, chaired around the ground by his team-mates, and waving with his good left arm to a generous reception even from the Sydneysiders who had read of his heroism in Brisbane.

'We just wanted him to know how we felt about him,' Murphy explained. 'We wouldn't have done it without him.'

In the crowd in Brisbane a couple of weeks earlier, Ned Kelly had slightly mixed feelings. 'Oh yeah, absolutely, from where we were standing you could see Prescott's arm was no good to him at all,' he confirms. 'I'll always remember him playing on, carrying his right arm and pretty much doing everything with his left. Huddart was brilliant too, he gave the Aussies all sorts of trouble. It was a great Test. But I did wonder, and this might sound bad but it's the way the game was played, why none of our forwards seemed to want to go near him. Let's not be polite, they should have attacked him. I couldn't think of a way he was still there at the end.'

Prescott conceded there was some quiet heroism, or at least chivalry, in the attitude of Australia's forwards.

'My opposing prop Brian Davies could have ruined my career and put me out of rugby for good if he had tried intentionally to have a go at my arm. He knew it was broken and that it was just hanging loosely outside the scrum. Brian McTigue, our other prop, and myself switched over at every scrum so that I didn't push with my right arm on the inside of the scrum. I was afraid of the pack collapsing on it. I will always be grateful to Brian Davies for leaving my arm alone.'

After the series was clinched in Sydney, the Lions went on to New Zealand. But Prescott did not play again for six months and retired from all rugby the following year. He had a briefly successful spell as the Saints coach, playing a key role in Ray French's transition from rugby union: 'He looked after me in my first year. He took me to one side, told me what to do. Just the simple things like play-the-balls - you had to do them properly in those days. He was always very concerned about his players. I found him a very good coach. Good for team spirit as well, a very jovial sort of fellow.

'I'll tell you how hard he was. I dislocated my shoulder playing for Saints at Swinton - they were a top side in those days. There were no subs, and with 15 or 20 minutes to go my shoulder had gone. I moved across to the right hand side of the field and had a word with Alan, told him it had gone - it really had, it was no use whatsoever. He just told me to pack on the blindside. And what else could you do but do as he said, after what he'd done in Brisbane?'

As Mitchell, the eccentric Cumbrian with whom he had struck up such a good relationship on that never-to-be-forgotten Lions tour, wrote in his own memoirs, published shortly before the pair died within two weeks of each other in September 1998, it was: '...selfless sacrifice for his team and country, unequalled in any sport anywhere in the world.'

● Andy Wilson admires the courage of anyone who plays rugby league at any level having dabbled in it at Leeds University. He has covered it for *The Observer* and *Guardian* since 1996, and written regularly for *League Express*, *League Weekly* and currently *Forty-20*.

11. Ahead of his Time

Mike Latham

WAR hero, Home Guard officer, scratch golfer, broadcaster, journalist, thespian, professional sprinter, restaurateur, self publicist, master tailor, devoted family man - Lancelot Beaumont Todd achieved many things in his life away from the rugby field.

But it is for his contributions to rugby league that he is best remembered, fondly to this day. As a player and later a manager he was inspirational and blessed with star quality. Todd, as he always reminded everyone, was the first overseas player, signing on for Wigan in 1908 four hours before his New Zealand team-mate George Smith signed on the dotted line for Oldham (after turning down Wigan's overtures).

After a break from the game, Todd re-emerged as manager of Salford in the interwar period, revitalising the club and presiding over their best ever period. He became one the sport's first broadcasters and had far-reaching ideas and visions for the game that went largely unheeded for decades. He was a superb judge of a player, knew how to put a team together and how to build success.

His death in a road accident in 1942 was widely mourned, but his name lives on in the Lance Todd Trophy, awarded to the Man of the Match in the Challenge Cup final. Visits to his gravestone in Wigan cemetery have become a regular pilgrimage for rugby league fans. Twice winner of the Lance Todd Trophy, Andy Gregory told me recently that, born and brought up close-by, he visits the grave on a regular basis, very much aware of Todd's huge contribution to the game's history.

Lancelot Beaumont Todd was born in Otahuhu in Auckland City in 1883. As a young adult he was a small, dapper man, 5ft 7in and ten stone, immaculately attired due perhaps to his training as a tailor. He played rugby from an early age and also developed a growing reputation as a 'cash' or professional sprinter. He once beat then world champion American Arthur Duffy (Olympic champion in 1900) off a two-and-a-half yards' start. On the rugby field he made up for his lack of height and weight with a remarkable eye for a gap which saw him cut through the strongest defences. His acceleration from a standing start gave him the edge over opponents. Moreover, he could read the game, dictate play and had a great rugby brain, qualities that served him well.

Todd's early career was spent with the Otahuhu club where his two elder brothers played and, in 1901, he joined the Suburbs club in Auckland at his father's suggestion. He soon made the first-team but then broke a collar bone on two occasions and was out of action for nearly a year on doctor's advice while he allowed those breaks to set. In 1905, he joined (Auckland) City club on the suggestion of their captain and All Black George Tyler. He played at five-eighth, displacing the New Zealand international Peter Ward and, when the rugby union All Blacks left for England, achieved Auckland Provincial honours.

In 1906, Todd joined Parnell because the Suburbs club had become extinct. At the end of that season he toured Australia with the Auckland City team, but had to come back early after suffering blood poisoning in his leg. He was in competition with many other talented players and struggled to earn further representative selection until he was invited for an All Black trial to play for North Island against South Island in 1907.

But Todd, unknown he thought to all but the promoters, had received an offer to join the professional All Blacks tour at the end of season. He refused, along with many other players, to sign an agreement not to travel if selected. For his refusal to sign, Todd was suspended by the Auckland union for three years without a hearing. The suspension was later extension into one for life, again without the option to present his case.

As we now know, Lance Todd did indeed join that famous tour to England, becoming one of the pioneers now better known as the All Golds in the process. Beforehand, he was considered an upcoming player, but he impressed as the trip wore on, appeared in all three Tests and became one of the mainstays of the side. His performances in its last month in particular were outstanding, as the fledgling Kiwis recovered from losing the first Test at Headingley to win the next two at Chelsea and Cheltenham and take the series.

The experience shaped Todd's whole approach to the

game. In an interview with the *Wigan Examiner* in April 1908 he said:

> Undoubtedly the feature of your game is the wonderfully fit condition of the Northern Union players. It was the one great surprise to our boys. The returned amateur All Blacks had spoken very poorly of the Northern Union play and players generally and we naturally thought we had more than an outside chance. I frankly confess that we were fairly staggered. Probably the old 'All Blacks' never saw a game and had swallowed all they were told.
>
> As to the game itself, I still think it is a great improvement on the old style and cannot imagine anything better from a spectator's point of view. For the players it certainly demands more preparation and I think getting into condition is one of the essentials for success.

Todd also revealed in the interview that he had helped tour promoter Albert Baskerville with his arrangements, an early sign that he had ambitions above and beyond being simply a player. He recruited several members of the side and told the story of one, un-named selection who pulled out of the tour party just before it was announced after receiving £70 to stay behind and continue his connection with the 'amateur' union.

It was very unusual for players to be directly quoted in newspaper articles or reports at this time and Todd's interview was a departure from the accepted norm. From the outset he was a strong personality with firm views and opinions, far from the subservient player that many professional football clubs expected.

Todd's displays captured the interest of Northern Union clubs and ambitious Wigan were an enthusiastic suitor.

Wigan had enjoyed a revival in their fortunes after moving to Central Park in 1902 and attracted large crowds that made their finances more secure. Todd signed in the dressing room after the final Test at Cheltenham on 15 February 1908, even though there was still one match of the tour remaining.

Prior to the tour the Northern Union clubs had made an agreement that the New Zealanders should not be approached until the conclusion of the official tour and there was some disquiet from outside that Wigan and Oldham had jumped the gun. Under the heading 'Colonial for Wigan, Todd signs on,' the *Wigan Examiner* reported that: 'Secretary Mr George Taylor and Director Mr James Henderson, representing the Central Park organisation, witnessed the third Test match at Cheltenham on Saturday and subsequently made terms with Todd, the necessary papers being signed the same evening.' They had also tried to sign Todd's friend and former club-mate George Smith, but he resisted Wigan's overtures and instead went to Oldham. Todd made a try-scoring Wigan debut four days later.

Smith, then 35, had signed for Oldham for a reported £150 but Todd's signature was reported to have cost £400, an amount which, according to one Manchester writer, was '...in accordance with Wigan's liberal traditions.' He added: "...the Wigan officials express themselves well satisfied with their enterprise. Todd usually played at five-eighth but in the last two games was placed at wing three-quarter and at both Chelsea and Cheltenham he showed resource and pace.'

Wigan agreed to support Todd in obtaining his tailoring diploma and he spent some time in London at Savile Row, Mayfair. He soon became part of Wigan's legendary three-quarter line of the Edwardian period, Leytham, Jenkins, Todd and Miller. Though the quartet was always referred to in that order Joe Miller was in fact the right-winger with Todd as his centre and Bert Jenkins and Jimmy Leytham on the left. Lancaster born Leytham was a gentlemanly winger and prolific try-scorer who met a tragic end in a boating accident on the River Lune in 1916. Jenkins was a rock-solid Welsh centre who provided the perfect foil for Leytham. Todd's partner was the only local from the quartet, Pemberton-born Miller, who lost little in comparison with Leytham in terms of try-scoring but was a very under-rated player.

Much later, in 1941, the *Wigan Examiner* veteran reporter Joe Leech reminisced about the qualities of each player - who between them scored 717 tries in 1,060 games:

> Leytham always acknowledged his debt to Jenkins, his brilliant partner. Leytham was a prolific scorer and probably the most popular player of his time in rugby league. Jenkins was a man of exceptionally powerful physique and a terror to opposing teams. Miller was the only Wiganer. A stockily-built player, he had a fine turn of speed and he developed a clever swerve which enabled him to elude opponents who had cut across the field.
>
> Todd was the idol of the crowd at Central Park and was induced to join Wigan at the conclusion of Baskerville's New Zealand tour in season 1907-08. One of the lightest three-quarters ever to represent Wigan he compensated for his lack of weight by superior skill and resource and was always a marked man. 'Toddy', as he was known, knew all the tricks. As a lightweight, he was easily thrown, when the opposing team could get at him, but he bounced like rubber and was soon up again and waiting for more. He could bluff cleverly and was an ideal partner for Miller. His passes were well-timed and, unless he was prevented from following-up, he was usually ready for a re-pass.'

The Northern Union game had only recently switched from 15 to 13-a-side and Wigan pioneered an exciting new approach to the game. Todd's signing was the forerunner of several new signings as Wigan's directors scoured the globe for talented players. Fellow New Zealanders Charlie Seeling, Massa Johnston, William Curran, Arthur Francis and Percy Williams were amongst those who followed Todd to Central Park, alongside a host of players from South Wales.

By the time Todd played his final first-team match for the club in November 1913 he had become a major celebrity in the town. The bald facts are that he played in 185 matches, scoring 126 tries and kicking seven goals. He shared in Wigan's inaugural Championship success in 1908-09 and was also a member of the first Wigan Challenge Cup Final line-up, losing to Broughton Rangers in 1911. During November 1910 he played twice for Lancashire alongside several other New Zealand born players and the Australian Mick Bolewski, who played for Leigh.

It was quickly apparent, however, that Todd was far from just a sportsman. He was a keen thespian and joined Wigan Little Theatre. When Wigan won the Lancashire Cup in 1908 a celebration dinner was arranged for the evening, but Todd was unable to attend as he had prior engagement as lead part in a theatrical production. He also opened a restaurant in Wigan town centre and, in May 1911, married the daughter, Ann Blaylock Samuels, of a prominent Wigan gentleman, Charley Samuels. The wedding was held at Wigan Parish Church. Like Todd, Samuels had been a former 'cash' sprinter and he had been a prominent member of the Wigan rugby side in the rugby union days, a big friend of the influential Jim Slevin, the borough electrical engineer and the first Wigan superstar footballer.

Todd also had a shrewd eye for his own worth and pulling power to a club attracting huge attendances. It was the custom for players in those days to receive a signing-on fee and effectively they would then be tied to the club for the rest of their career or until the directors (who also picked the side) saw fit to transfer them. Not so with Todd. He only ever signed for one season at a time, negotiating a new signing-on fee each time.

In May 1909, Todd's adoring Wigan public awoke to the news in the *Wigan Examiner* - Todd's mouthpiece - that he was to return home for good in the next month or so. Todd had been upset towards the end of the season that he had been dropped from some games in favour of the Welshman Gomer Gunn, a player he considered far inferior to himself. He hired a public hall to explain his decision and 2,000 Wigan supporters turned up to hear him speak.

Todd stayed around until just before the start of the next season before setting off home, arriving in New Zealand in September 1909. He then conducted negotiations with the Wigan officials by cablegram. His brinksmanship worked as he was made an offer to return and came back in November 1909, re-signing for a reported £250 fee. When Todd arrived at Plymouth on the steamship *Arawa*, a deputation of four Wigan officials was waiting at the dockside to greet him. They then proceeded to London by train, where they enjoyed a production at Drury Lane theatre, before continuing their journey to Wigan the following day. When Todd arrived back, a massive crowd gathered on Wallgate to greet him as he emerged from the railway station and he spoke to the assembled throng.

Todd was never shy of publicity throughout his time in the town and was often the mouthpiece for the players, complaining to the officials on one occasion when they only received sandwiches after a long rail trip to Hunslet. After Wigan's victory in the Lancashire Cup final in December 1912, he took the opportunity to speak to supporters at the celebration dinner held that evening at the Minorca Hotel.

Todd again mentioned the fact that he was the oldest colonial in the game, having signed on four hours before Smith and he never regretted coming to Wigan.

'It is likely I will be leaving you in the course of a few months,' he added, 'but I trust that Charlie Seeling and Percy Williams will maintain the reputation of the club. My heart will always be with you and I will be eager to learn in Auckland how you are faring. As to the Wigan team, each member is one of the 13 and that is why we won our games.'

Following an altercation with a committee member (Todd claimed he was insulted by the member) he said in December 1913 that he would not play for them again. The dispute was apparently resolved, but Todd only played in the reserve team and was transfer-listed at £400 in January 1914.

His destination was Dewsbury, for whom he made his debut against Hull KR on 17 January 1914.

Todd's popularity stayed high with Wigan supporters and some club members called a general meeting to express their dissatisfaction with his transfer and the manner of his departure from Wigan. The meeting, held at the Co-operative Hall, was described as 'disorderly' and at one stage the Wigan committee walked off the platform en masse after being roundly barracked. Todd was present, but was refused permission to speak as club officials stated he was no longer a member and not entitled to do so. When the meeting broke up in disarray, Todd then took his opportunity to take to the floor to loud cries of 'Well played, Dewsbury!'

Todd insisted he had a right to be there, so that any mis-statements on either side might be contradicted. The committee had treated him with contempt and if they were not men enough to remain on the platform, he had nothing to say for or against them. Doubtless, there were faults on either side. Perhaps he had been bad to manage and they were bad managers, but when a player had a grievance and took it to the committee he had a right to be heard. He was sorry to be leaving the club but had not left the town. There was no doubting where the affections of the Wigan supporters lay.

Todd played eleven times, scoring three tries before the end of the season, but his days at Dewsbury were not particularly happy. When Wigan visited Crown Flatt the travelling supporters were dismayed to learn that Todd was not in the home line-up. It emerged that a deputation of Dewsbury players had met the directors prior to the game and presented a petition that stated Todd should be dropped from the side '...as his performances did not merit his inclusion.' The directors agreed and Todd was left out. When news of this decision became known, many of the home fans barracked their own players and directors throughout the match in scenes described as 'increasingly ugly.'

With war clouds threatening, football matters soon went on the back burner as the grim realities of the rapidly worsening international situation dominated attention. Little was then heard of Todd until a report appeared in the *Sporting Chronicle* (24 August 1916). This stated that obituaries for rugby union players were common in the leading 'class' papers (like *The Times*) but Northern Union players were not mentioned. It went on: 'The Northern Union man is not in the way of gaining a commission like his rugby union counterparts. His education and vocation have not fitted him to pass the tests necessary to be an officer. Exceptions are Lieutenant Gwyn Thomas and Lieutenant LB Todd, but generally speaking the numbers are few.'

'Second-Lieut Lancelot B Todd, the famous New Zealand footballer, has been promoted lieutenant,' reported the *Wigan Examiner* in April 1916. 'He joined a contingent of New Zealanders and saw service in Gallipoli, where he was given his commission.' Todd later rose to the rank of captain.

With World War One over, Todd began a new life as secretary at the Blackpool North Shore Golf Club. There were 487 applications for the position, which carried a salary of £250 per annum. He took over his new post in September 1921 and stayed on the Fylde Coast for several years. Occasionally reports appeared in local newspapers stating he had been successful in winning golf competitions. Todd planned to return to New Zealand in the late 1920s, but delayed that due to his wife being unwell. In July 1928 he read an advertisement from Salford for the post of secretary-manager and successfully applied for the job.

Todd took up his duties at Salford on 1 August 1928, and was an instant success, taking the club from 26th in the league, prior to his arrival, to fourth position in his first season. In November 1933 he signed a new, seven-year contract agreement and stayed at the Willows until after the outbreak of the Second World War.

During his time with Salford, Todd oversaw a remarkable run of success as his charges won the Lancashire Cup for the first time in the club's history, defeating Swinton in the 1931 final and going on to repeat the success on three more occasions. Salford won the Championship three times, in 1933, 1937 and 1939 and were runners-up once (to Todd's old club Wigan in 1934).

On the latter occasion, following Wigan's 15-3 victory, Todd entered the Wigan motor-coach just as it was about to leave the Warrington ground and addressed the players. 'Congratulations to the Wigan team from an old Wigan player,' he said. "You have been the better team today. If we are in the final again next year I hope we shall beat you. If we are not in the first four I hope you will win the Cup again.'

Salford lifted the Challenge Cup at Wembley in 1938, defeating Barrow. They returned to the capital the following year but their side was stricken with a flu virus before the game and lost to Halifax. They did recover remarkably, however, to defeat Castleford in the Championship at Maine Road the following week before a crowd of over 69,000, just as war clouds were looming again.

In 1934, the fledgling French Rugby League invited Salford to undertake a promotional six-match tour in an attempt to publicise the game across the Channel. The trip was a huge success and Salford's team proved to be perfect ambassadors for the game. They were dubbed 'Les Diables Rouges' or 'the Red Devils' by the French journalists, a nickname that survived through the years and has indeed now been appended officially in Super League.

Assessing Todd's contribution to the Salford success, respected club historian Graham Morris says: 'When Todd arrived at Salford some of the future stars were already there - players like Barney Hudson and Billy Williams, for example - but he extracted the very best out of the talent he had at his disposal and moulded them into a fine side. His lengthy absence from the game had not impaired his judgement.

'Todd built a side based on flair and imagination and transformed the mood around the club virtually overnight from gloom to glory. In his first season he only added two players to the squad, but their change in fortunes was remarkable. He was particularly good at spotting which rugby union players, especially Welsh ones, would be able to make the transition to rugby league. He set up a network of scouts throughout the country and got regular tips and reports sent through to him. But he always insisted on watching the player himself, often more than on one occasion, before he signed them.

'Todd signed some remarkably talented players from Welsh rugby union, players like Gus Risman, Emlyn Jenkins, Billy Watkins, Alan Edwards and Bert Day, but also had an eye elsewhere - the fullback Harold Osbaldestin from the Wigan area for example and the Cumbrian Sammy Miller.

'I don't think Todd actually coached the side,' Morris continues. 'The composition of teams was very different in those days. He signed the players, organised them, made all the arrangements for training and matches, but he had a trainer to get them fit and keep them that way. Tactics, such as they were, were largely determined by a few of the senior players before a game. But Todd left no one in any doubt that he was in charge. He was the motivator before matches and Emlyn Jenkins once told me that Todd could change a game at half-time with one of his speeches in the dressing room.

'He presided over The Willows from his office in the old pavilion and always seemed to be at the ground at all hours of day and night. He was a very smart man, usually seen in a suit with waistcoat and watch-chain, and his hair immaculately groomed.

'Players I spoke to of that era said that he immediately commanded respect, but that he was also a very fair and kindly man. He looked after the players, made sure that off the field they had decent places to live, that their families were settled in the area. If one was ill or injured, Todd would make sure they got the best medical attention. He was regarded as a father figure by his players.'

A Testimonial match was given in Lance Todd's honour to acknowledge his ten years service to the club, the idea coming from the Salford Supporters' Association. In the programme notes, the man himself singled out the club's win at Wembley in 1938 as his greatest moment. 'It was the culmination of years of hard work and the realisation of the dream of everybody connected with the club,' he wrote.

Todd's contract with Salford was not renewed when it expired on 9 November 1940, due to the uncertain situation regarding the war.

'It was ironic that the First World War effectively ended his playing career and the Second World War ended his managerial career,' Morris says. 'Quite what he would have achieved but for the war is anyone's guess, but he had the knowledge and the intuition to re-shape the Salford side and bring in new players as and when required.'

While at Salford, Todd branched out. He wrote newspaper articles about the sport and became a pioneering radio broadcaster. His articles were widely read and discussed and he was never afraid to ruffle feathers. 'In many ways Todd was a man ahead of his time,' Morris points out. 'Even in the early 1930s, for example, Todd was advocating summer rugby league.'

An article from the *Wigan Examiner* of 11 July 1931 demonstrates Todd's far-sighted approach. Entitled: 'Summer Rugby - LB Todd's Revolutionary Proposals - Wigan unfavourable,' the article showed Todd's far-thinking, but also the opposition he met with his attempts at change:

> Lance Todd has dropped a bombshell into sporting circles by suggesting that the Rugby League should abandon winter football and play the game in summer. Briefly, Mr Todd's revolutionary proposals are: Season to start on a Saturday nearest to March 1st and extend to early November; close-season to part of November and the whole of December, January and

February. In March, April, October and November time to kick-off 3-30pm. In May, June, July, August and September kick-off about 7-30pm.

The advantages claimed by Mr Todd are: avoiding postponed matches for bad weather - there were nearly one hundred last season; affording entertainment for thousands at a loose end on summer evenings; supporters would accompany their teams in large numbers; evening training for players; economy in protecting grounds from severe weather; four months absolutely clear of Soccer opposition.

One of the leading writers of the day, 'Forward' in the *Athletic News*, canvassed opinions about Todd's proposals. 'Some are inclined to ridicule the suggestions, but I found a surprising level of support,' he wrote. 'One level-headed club official said the period from November to February was a veritable nightmare for clubs and he would support the change to relieve himself of this burden.

'But should the miracle happen and the principle of summer football be approved, what then? Is the Rugby League prepared to stand alone as the one sport indifferent to the established and legitimate claims of every other? I am told that the Rugby League, in effect, stands alone. Mr John Wilson (Secretary of the RFL) says he will be sorry to see rugby league football encroaching on summer games. And so will every real sportsman.'

The *Wigan Examiner*'s rugby writer, 'Referee' was more scathing. 'A good many people in Wigan are not inclined to take the proposal seriously,' he wrote. 'Coming from such a publicist as 'LB' one is not surprised at this view.' He went on:

Personally, I have never heard of such a revolutionary proposal connected with any sport and I doubt whether the proposal will ever take practical shape. Rugby is essentially a winter pastime and there is not the least likelihood of rugby union clubs following the League's example if they were foolish enough to adopt summer rugby.

The brilliant work Mr Todd has accomplished for the Salford club is its own answer to the scheme. If the clubs adopt a go-ahead policy and provide the right type of football, then rugby league will prosper in winter. I have spoken to several members of the Wigan directorate who regard the idea as impracticable, and have not the least doubt that this will be the general view. There are sports for summer quite enough to satisfy without the encroachment of professional rugby. Let us think of those who play, watch and enjoy those games and be a little less selfish!

In 1996, over 60 years after Todd's ideas were first put forward, rugby league made the switch to summer.

In May 1937, Salford travelled to Leeds to play in an experimental 12-a-side exhibition game. The idea came from Lance Todd with each pack scrimmaging in a 2-3 formation. The entry of the ball into the scrum was improved and made play quicker but the radical step was never adopted.

When the Second World War began, Todd joined the Salford Home Guard and soon became second in command. He combined that role by maintaining his interest in rugby. In November 1940, the England-Wales wartime international at Oldham had radio commentary by Todd. His knowledge of the game shone through his commentaries and he received many complimentary letters and comments from listeners.

In February 1942, the legendary Wigan full-back Jim Sullivan was the subject of a BBC Radio broadcast in the *Giants of Sport* series, hosted by Victor Smythe, a well-known

Manchester-based broadcaster and presenter of the period. Sullivan was interviewed by Todd who told him: 'I'll pay you this compliment. I've seen you as the Rock of Gibraltar - if ever a man has an example to set to young players that man is you.'

Tragically, Lance Todd was killed in a road accident on Saturday 14 November 1942, when the car he was in hit an electric tram standard. Todd, then 59, was with his commanding officer, Lieutenant Colonel PR Sewell, who also died in the accident on Manchester Road, Oldham. It has been said they were returning from a match. His daughter was interviewed in May 2004 and she said they had tried to avoid a boy who lost control of his bike and was wobbling in the road.

The Lance Todd Man of the Match award for the Challenge Cup final was instituted by the Australian journalist and former tour and Wigan team manager Harry Sunderland, a friend of Todd's, Warrington director Bob Anderton, who had been tour manager 1932 and 1936 and *Yorkshire Evening Post* journalist John B Bapty, who wrote under the name of 'Little John.' First awarded in 1946, the award was to be decided by votes cast by the press (and from its formation in 1961, members of the Rugby League Writers Association) present at the game.

The Red Devils Association was founded in 1953 by Gus Risman, Barney Hudson, Emlyn Jenkins and Billy Williams, and open to players who had played for Todd. At their meeting on 12 May 1956, it was proposed by Jimmy Lindley that a donation of £25 be made to purchase a permanent trophy for presentation to the winner of the Lance Todd award at Wembley, plus a replica to be retained by the player. It was decided to invite the recipient to the Red Devils reunion each year to receive his trophy, an event that has been a focal point of the evening ever since. The first player honoured was Leeds scrum-half Jeff Stevenson in 1957.

Todd's emotional interment at Wigan Cemetery following a joint memorial service (for himself and Lieut-Col Sewell) in Salford was attended by thousands of mourners. His coffin was draped in the Union Jack and the bearers were members of the Wigan Battalion of the Home Guard. Many of his former team-mates, including Kiwi Charlie Seeling were present. The Home Guard detachment fired three volleys over the grave and then buglers sounded the 'Last Post' and the *Reveille*. There will never be his like again.

● Mike Latham has spent much of the past 40 years researching the history of rugby league in libraries. Consequently he wears glasses and blinks in daylight. He has written over 20 books and is back writing the Leigh programme after a 20-year gap. He is chairman of the Association of Sports Historians and also chairman of cricket for Cumberland CCC.

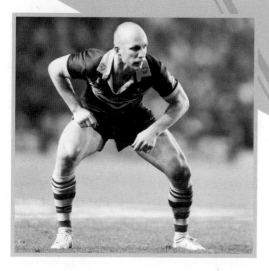

12. It Ain't Over 'til It's Over

Christopher Irvine

IN the Australian winter of 2014 something truly remarkable happened. New South Wales, poor downtrodden New South Wales, ended eight years of torment in State of Origin.

Queensland, mighty Queensland, were finally vanquished. Sydney erupted. Fireworks exploded above the Harbour Bridge. Cameron Smith, Johnathan Thurston, Greg Inglis and Co looked desolate, their dynasty ended. Among them on the pitch at the end was a resolutely upright figure who Mal Meninga, as coach of the Maroons, would probably have still chucked a jumper to, had this man not rung the curtain down on his own extraordinary career some three years earlier.

13 Inspirations

Looking at this fit, sharp-suited, shaven-headed demigod, consoling the players on one hand while extracting their live gut reaction for Channel 9 on the other, you could not help but wonder whether he would have made the difference had he still been playing. Toss him a pair of boots and watch him inspire.

Simply, Darren Lockyer was born to win - and born to lead, as it turned out. Queensland's eight-year Origin stranglehold began under his captaincy in 2006, New South Wales having gone one-nil up in Sydney as the Blues bore down on an unprecedented [at that stage] fourth successive series triumph. There were calls for Lockyer's head. Meninga wanted to shift him to full-back, but Lockyer dug his heels in to stay and steer the Queensland ship from stand-off. Meninga stuck by his man and the Maroons walloped their rivals 30-6 in game two. They were 14-4 down in the decider when Lockyer, not normally one for talking let alone swearing, gathered his players and said: 'There is still time to win. We're Queenslanders, we don't fucking give up.'

Johnathan Thurston, who Lockyer had a quiet word with about lifting his head up, saw his chance, stepping the cover in dispatching the unstoppable Brent Tate. Queensland were two points down with just over a couple of minutes on the clock, when Lockyer pushed the ball deep more in hope than expectation. Eric Grothe gathered but from the subsequent play-the-ball Brett Hodgson, normally so dependable cleaning up at the back, sent a pass beyond the reach of another future Warrington favourite Matt King. It was right place, right time for Lockyer - a recurring theme throughout his career - who seized the ball on the bounce and skipped over for the winning try. An era of Queensland greatness had begun, with Lockyer the beating heart of what proved for years to be an unbeatable team.

In the 'show us yer medals' stakes alone, Lockyer would get my 'best player I ever saw' award. Jonathan Davies and Martin Offiah would be right up there, along with a raft of Antipodeans in Mal Meninga, Laurie Daley, Allan Langer, Andrew Johns, Billy Slater, Johnathan Thurston, Lesley Vainikolo and Stacey Jones, but the purring sleekness of Lockyer set him apart for this onlooker.

He is rugby league's equivalent of Roger Federer - impeccably cool, resolutely unflustered, and unerring in pretty much everything he does. Above all, he is a classicist. Just as Federer operates in his own bubble, Lockyer worked inside his personal force field. He engineered the time and space to touch the tiller at precisely the correct moment, wave his wand of a boot, or execute just the right pass. His single-minded pursuit of perfection drove him. As much as he tormented Great Britain and England, no-one watching Lockyer could do anything but express admiration. He could have stuck a warning sign in the ground for opponents - 'Beware, genius at work'.

Robbie Hunter-Paul was early in his own international career with New Zealand when he first came up against Lockyer at North Harbour Stadium in Auckland in 1998. 'It was a typical Auckland day, the rain pouring and the ground saturated,' Hunter-Paul said. 'We Kiwis knew what we had to do to the young Aussie guy who came on at full-back. Pump the ball his way every time. We kicked off long and the new kid dropped it. On two occasions he ran the ball out, got chopped down and lost possession. He couldn't hold the pill in the wet. That sort of experience can faze a player but not him.

'Even in a match Australia lost, there were a few things Darren Lockyer did that got you thinking that here was someone special. We were still ahead with five minutes to go when I made a break. There wasn't a full-back in England at that time that I couldn't leave for dead, but not this guy. Twenty metres out, I came off my left foot, then off my right and somehow he got me.

'Even when he was bad, the fact is Lockyer was better than most. The best player of all time? I can't say. But he was certainly the best player I faced in my era, one quite freakish in his ability. He was consistent - consistently lethal. To play the level he did for a decade and a half is extraordinary. Maybe in the last couple of years his star waned a bit in physical terms, including the most vicious of sidesteps. But he remained a tactical and visionary genius, as well as an inspirational captain.'

Brad Walter, *Sydney Morning Herald* correspondent, tells a story about Lockyer after that Test match in 1998. Lockyer was in the team hotel foyer at 4am waiting for a taxi to take him to the airport for his early flight back to Brisbane and a game for the Broncos the next day. 'The first sign for me that he was made of sterner stuff was his reaction when a group of media entered the foyer,' Walter said. 'While many people would have had their head down and tried to ignore a journalist who had just written their international rugby league obituary, Lockyer at least offered some acknowledgement.

'He'd come on for Robbie O'Davis. He'd made mistake after mistake in that match, dropping passes, spilling bombs, fumbling grubbers, falling off tackles, to virtually gift the Kiwis their win that day. By his own admission, and that of others involved in the Kangaroos' 22-16 loss to New Zealand, the 21-year-old full-back had just turned in one of the worst performances seen in the green and gold of Australia. Whether he would ever recover was a question on many people's lips that night. Some players after making it to Test or State of Origin level have crumbled under the pressure and then barely been sighted again. At the time, few of us could imagine that Lockyer would play for Australia again, let alone go on to become the most capped player in Test history. As we came to learn, Lockyer wasn't one of those players. The next day he turned in an absolute blinder for Brisbane.'

Six months later, Lockyer scored tries and landed a combined seven goals as Australia swept aside the Kiwis, first in Brisbane and a week later at the scene of his disastrous official Test debut at North Harbour Stadium. His unofficial international debut had come a year previously in a Super League Test against New Zealand, in which he scored twice in another beaten cause, and subsequent series with Great Britain, aged 20, two years after his 'rookie of the year' first junior season at Brisbane Broncos. The bitter Super League war and splitting of the game down under had opened the international door for a prodigious talent. He grabbed his chance with both soft hands. Even then Lockyer was being talked about in the pantheon of great Australian full-backs: Clive Churchill, Graeme Langlands, Greg Brentnall, Garry Jack, Gary Belcher and Brett Mullins. At a time, too, when Australia were hardly short of options in the No 1 position, from Wendell Sailor, David Peachey, Ken Nagas and Robbie Ross to the then Australia Rugby League-affiliated Robbie O'Davis and Tim Brasher.

The golden boy inevitably attracted the attention of the British media, whose admiration for Lockyer never once wavered during the 15 years he kept putting Great Britain and England to the sword right up until the Four Nations final of 2011. There was a typically cautious but prescient comment in those early days from Wayne Bennett, his coach and mentor at the Broncos: 'He has shown how good he is at the moment. How far he will go depends on how he handles the success he is having now. There are things he has to get in place and keep in place over the years. He might not even finish his career at full-back.'

Lockyer was six years away from his incarnation as a stand-off, however you sensed what Bennett foresaw: a full-back with a creative vision to direct play and vary attacking angles. Indeed, Lockyer spent much of his youth playing at No 6, although had the family not moved to the Queensland country outpost of Roma it might have been a different story altogether. David, his father, loved Australian Rules, as well as being a handy soccer player. Growing up in Brisbane, Lockyer's first sporting steps were playing for the Springwood junior AFL club. It was only when the family relocated to Wandoan, a small community in the Western Downs region five hours north of Brisbane, that he discovered rugby league. A further move to the country outpost of Roma, when Lockyer was starting high school, saw him flourish in getting his first taste of representative rugby league in the Queensland Under 12s squad at centre alongside Elton Flatley, who went on to play rugby union for Australia.

It helped, too, that the only game in town was rugby league in Roma, which has produced the likes of the great Arthur Beetson, Brent Tate and Willie Carne. It was aged 14 that Lockyer was spotted by Cyril Connell who was, 'quite simply the best man I have ever met in my time in football,' Lockyer said in his highly-acclaimed autobiography. Connell retired as Broncos recruitment manager at the same time Wayne Bennett left the Broncos in 2008. Aged 80, his own legend had been burnished by the players he scouted and recruited for the club: Wendell Sailor, Lote Tuqiri, Justin Hodges, Shane Webcke, Petero Civoniceva, Tonie Carroll,

Darius Boyd, Steve Renouf, Karmichael Hunt, Shaun Berrigan, Brad Thorn, Sam Thaiday, Corey Parker, Dane Carlaw, Brent Tate ... the list goes on.

Connell, the Broncos' so-called 'gold miner', introduced himself to Lockyer at an Under 15s carnival at Caboolture, when the youngster was playing for the South West region. He told Lockyer he liked what he saw and that he would be keeping a close on his development. It was all the incentive a lad with professional aspirations needed. He received a scholarship and a place in the Broncos Colts for the 1995 season. As part of the contract he signed at the age of 16, he was given a job behind the bar of the Broncos leagues club. His relationship remained a close one up to Connell's death.

'A nod and a wink was worth a thousand words to the pair of them,' according to Bennett, who three months into Lockyer's apprenticeship at the club wandered over to him during a training session and informed him that he would be part of the first grade squad to play Parramatta Eels that weekend. If the legend was not quite born that afternoon - he did lay on a try for Steve Renouf in coming off the bench in an otherwise routine win - it was the first step on a path extending through to 468 career appearances and scoring 1,598 points (174 tries, 438 goals and 26 drop-goals) for Brisbane, Queensland and Australia.

Lockyer was far from an unknown quantity when Australia's Super League side arrived in England in 1997. The youngster had laid down his marker against British clubs in the grimly one-sided World Club Championship, which Brisbane won that year. In a representative side replete with star names, the likes of Laurie Daley, Andrew Ettingshausen, Brett Mullins, Bradley Clyde, Steve Walters and Gorden Tallis, Lockyer first learned the happy knack of foiling Great

Britain and later England in a final match decider. With his considerable winnings that first year proper, thanks to the Super League revolution, he helped buy his parents' house in Roma and his own home.

A young man with the world at his feet made the first of 36 State of Origin appearances for Queensland in 1998, a series the Maroons won 2-1. Brisbane backed up their 1997 Super League Premiership with another a year later in a side he rated the best he played in: Darren Lockyer; Wendell Sailor, Darren Smith, Steve Renouf, Michael Hancock; Kevin Walters, Allan Langer; Shane Webcke, Phillip Lee, Andrew Gee, Gorden Tallis, Brad Thorn, Tonie Carroll. Substitutes: Kevin Campion, Petero Civoniceva, Peter Ryan, John Plath.

However, he remained adamant that representing Australia was not just an honour and privilege, but the crowning achievement of his playing career. He was the thorn in Great Britain's side during the 1999 Tri-series Down Under, scoring two tries in a 42-6 hiding on his home turf at the former Lang Park and again facing England at Twickenham in the opening match of the 2000 World Cup. His try and four goals helped beat the Kiwis 40-12 in the World Cup final at Old Trafford. He was in only two losing sides against Britain, the first at Huddersfield in the opening encounter of the 2001 Ashes series and again in Sydney, when Britain enjoyed another of those now all too rare one-off victories over the Kangaroos in the 2006 Tri Nations. The Kiwis ensured, however, that Lockyer, far from always having things his own way, had to endure the agonies of losing both the 2008 World Cup final and 2010 Four Nations final in his beloved Suncorp Stadium backyard.

Being handed the Test captaincy by Chris Anderson as coach in 2003 - curiously, he was third choice to succeed Brad Fittler after injuries befell Andrew Johns and Gorden

Tallis - changed Lockyer both as a player and person. For a record 34 Tests, Australia had no need to look elsewhere for their inspirational leader. The office of captain was one he took immensely seriously in turning to Ricky Ponting and George Gregan, respective Australia cricket and rugby union captains at the time, as role models. He approached the job with due gravitas in setting an example for all players in Australia to follow. When Cameron Smith eventually succeeded him, there was a real season of Lockyer's values being passed on, moreover to a fellow Queenslander and valued team-mate. Understandably, Lockyer liked that.

New in the job in 2003, he could not have been more accommodating. Before the Test series, the media were invited to spend a convivial dinner with the Kangaroos at their Leeds hotel. The evening ended with a quiz and I found myself on Lockyer's team. Put it this way, he knew his rugby league history. Even in that relaxed atmosphere, you could sense his urgency to win. Inevitably, thanks to him, we did. There was also a sweepstake for the overnight Melbourne Cup. A few of us met up with Lockyer at training the next day. 'How did you get on in the Melbourne Cup Darren?' 'I won.' Of course he did. If you encountered him on tour walking around Leeds or Manchester, he would always stop for a chat. There were no airs or graces, just the humility of a guy content to go about his business, yet driven by a personal mission to be the best he could. Not every Australia captain had the British media eating out of his hand; Lockyer did. It was hard not to like him and impossible not to admire him.

Lockyer's Kangaroos were pushed all the way in the three matches but still completed a whitewash that year. In the last few minutes of each game, they found a way to win. The 2004 Tri Nations final at Elland Road was a Lockyer tour de force like no other on British soil. By now he had made a permanent switch to stand-off as the puppetmaster. Brian Noble's Great Britain side went into that showdown with a real sense that it was their time to end more than 30 years of hurt against the Aussies. Lockyer had received the Golden Boot for the first time as world player of the year in 2003. A year later the award went to longstanding Britain captain Andrew Farrell in the week of the final. It was to be Farrell's last game before a move to rugby union. My personal recollection of that night is BBC commentator Ray French nudging me before the game, convinced himself that Britain were going to do it. As French grimly muttered a couple of hours later: 'Bloody Lockyer!'

The bald statistics were a Lockyer try and six goals in a 44-4 victory. He had not played since aggravating a rib injury that caused him to miss a narrow win and loss in the two preceding group games against Britain. Get into Lockyer's ribs was Britain's battlecry, yet they rarely laid a finger on him. Lockyer dissected Noble's team with surgical precision, plunging the knife in deeper and deeper. The Kangaroos led 38-0 by half-time, their captain having had a hand in five tries, in addition to his own dazzling 60-metre score. As the orchestrator of Britain's torment, once again, Lockyer was humble in his assessment: it was all down to the team. Yes, but the team followed their brilliant baton twirler on a night when he left the home side bewitched, bothered and bewildered.

It was a theme repeated throughout Lockyer's international career. Great Britain or England were kept at arm's length, but the Kiwis did eventually get to him and his Australia team. The 2008 World Cup final was a chastening experience for a player who had already clocked up two Golden Boots, four Premierships with Brisbane and was well into Queensland's eight-year State of Origin monopoly.

International success was almost a given, but once Lockyer exposed his own human susceptibility in letting a ball bobble out of his hands that would have put Australia 16-0 up, New Zealand pounced. Moreover, it was a New Zealand side with Wayne Bennett in their camp. As Lockyer later recounted, it was a victory with 'Wayne's fingerprints all over it.' Self-belief carried the Kiwis home that night. That defeat cut deep - it doubtless still irks him - even though it was a rivalry the international game badly needed at that time.

For all his driven nature to win, Lockyer always saw the wider picture. He was tempted but never played club rugby here - Widnes had a go at persuading him to have one more season, but Lockyer politely declined the Vikings' invitation - yet he remained a committed advocate of the international game, unlike far too many of his compatriots.

The end of the road for him as a player was always penciled in for Elland Road - where else? - and the Four Nations final at the climax of an emotional farewell season. The fanfares were long and loud. In State of Origin, Queensland's dominance was duly maintained. His golden point kick, in defiance of a fractured cheekbone and in his last Brisbane appearance as it turned out, took the Broncos into the semis-finals past Wayne Bennett's St George Illawarra Dragons, and 2011, inevitably and conclusively, led to the home of Leeds United.

When Lockyer first played at Elland Road in the winning decider of the 1997 Super League Test series, Leeds United finished fifth in the Premier League that season. Things looked rather different back there in 2011, with Leeds in mid-table obscurity in the second-tier Championship and the ground, similarly, peeling at the edges. Lockyer's own journey in that time took him from bolter to icon. In the build-up to a final, for which England qualified with a resounding win over New Zealand, there was really only talk about one man. Early on in that week he spoke with the British media in that familiar wheezy, husky growl of his that somehow forces people to take notice. One journalist described him as the 'Australian Godfather', a voice that Lockyer had lived with for seven years after a big hit to the throat left a bone stuck in his larynx.

As always, though, his words rang with striking clarity, if not his damaged vocal chords. 'I pinch myself and ask myself, "how did I do that?",' he said. 'When you get to the end, it does feel like it's gone in a blink of an eye. Seventeen years ago, if you said you'd play this many games with this team and that team, I'd have thought you were dreaming. It's just been a hell of a ride, but it's coming to an end now and I just feel blessed the time I've had. I've had a bit of practice with the last game thing over in Australia, at Origin and club level. With every game the focus has always been the footy. The fact it's my last game and there's so much at stake allows you to distance yourself from the emotion.

'I guess knowing it's my last season I wanted to make sure I enjoyed it. To do that I've made sure I've worked hard at everything. It's been about giving everything and not having any regrets. You can't leave anything in the tank. I want to be on the plane back knowing I did all I could. I know it will be my last game of rugby league but all you can do is prepare for this one last match. There will be nerves, there always are before big games. Every game you fear failure. But you prepare the best you can and you give the best performance you can. The outcome looks after itself.

'But saying all that, I still pinch myself. Growing up, I dreamed of playing for Brisbane Broncos and maybe one day representing Queensland. Even as a kid, though, I'd seen the green and gold as the highest honour. I know State of

Origin is big back home, but I remember getting up early to watch the Kangaroos play Great Britain in Ashes series. To wear the jersey is a great reward for your efforts as a player, but it's also a responsibility to represent your country. That's something I've never taken lightly, or taken for granted.'

For a final time, Lockyer and his Kangaroos excelled when it mattered most, England suffering again at the hands of a maestro and his pitch-perfect players. Lockyer's destiny was always to finish a winner and he had the last but one word with Australia's 79th-minute fifth try of a 30-8 victory. His stabbed kick through rebounded off a post protector and sat up perfectly, as if the rugby gods wanted to bestow one last favour. The last word was his conversion attempt from in front of the posts, which skewed off the outside of his boot. Frailty had its say at the conclusion of a glorious career. At the end of the after-match press conference, journalists stood and applauded Lockyer. That just does not happen to anyone.

The Australian media manager instructed that there would be no one-on-one interviews, but that was never Lockyer's style. He was still politely answering questions long into that last night. His very last interview as a player was with the ubiquitous Australian journalist Steve Mascord, who asked for one memory from the night and promised he would then leave him in peace. 'It's hard to pinpoint,' Lockyer said, 'but when we ran out and the national anthems were being sung, I've never seen that many England flags just waving. I've played here a few times and that's probably the best atmosphere I've experienced here at Elland Road. So it was a great, great night.'

It was the perfect finish for a copper-bottomed legend of the sport, now one cast in bronze outside the magnificent Suncorp Stadium in Brisbane, home to his beloved Broncos. A short punt away is the statue of Wally Lewis, Lockyer's boyhood idol, whom his father took him to meet when he was 12. 'Like all dads, he just wanted his kids to do well,' Lockyer said, at the unveiling of his statute in 2012. 'I idolised Wally Lewis as the King. To get to meet him was a massive day in my life. To wind the clock forward 20 years and to be here is very special me.'

For all Lockyer's commentary work and ambassadorial roles - there was never any real need to fall back on his carpentry apprenticeship - life for this father of three sons will probably never again have the same acutely sharp focus that comes when playing at the top of your game and at such heady heights for the sustained period he did. Not that the fires still don't burn.

When Queensland lost their Origin stranglehold in 2014, you could see the great man's pain. His legend lives on.

● Chris Irvine began reporting on rugby league for *The Times* in 1992. He also provides coverage for the *Sunday Times* while force feeding sports journalism students a rugby league diet as a senior lecturer at the University of Huddersfield.

13. The Mike Gregory Way

Dave Hadfield

IT says a lot about the sport of rugby league that such a range of candidates spring to mind when you reflect on the people who have inspired you.

The first great players I noticed, perhaps; the likes of Billy Boston or Alex Murphy? Albert Fearnley and Bak Diabira at Blackpool Borough? Arthur Beetson in Australia? Or Phil Clarke, not for his mind-numbing number-crunching on Sky, but for the way he responded to a career-ending broken neck by building three other careers.

Then there's someone like a lad who plays for my local amateur team, who turns up every week and makes 50 tackles with an increasingly creaky body, has a few pints and goes home - all for nothing but the love of the game. He's an inspiration as well.

But, however I look at it, I keep coming back to one name - Mike Gregory. I have known nobody braver, on or off the field, and I am proud to have known him.

I wish the circumstances had been different, though. Yes, I'd always 'known' Mike as one of the very best players and coaches in the game, as well as one of the most outgoing and magnetic personalities. If there was a laugh to be had, Michael Gregory would be in the vicinity, more often than not at the epicentre.

What was happening to Mike in 2004, however, was no laughing matter. He had got what he called his dream job, coaching his hometown team, Wigan, but almost immediately things had started to go badly wrong. What was happening to him would have been cruel in the case of an average citizen. For someone as devoted to fitness and athleticism as him it must have been doubly unbearable.

I first became aware of Mike Gregory as a young loose forward at Warrington, fresh from the prolific rugby league nursery that is Wigan St Patricks, blond hair flapping and making him instantly recognisable. I think it was one of his few regrets that he never played for Wigan, although there is a certain irony in that, given what happened later.

Greg hit the ground running at Wilderspool, making his debut at 18 and playing in a Lancashire Cup final victory over St Helens in only his tenth game. Apart from natural ability, which he had in abundance, the prime reason for him making such a swift transition from amateur youth rugby to the tough, sometimes violent world of professional rugby league was his attitude to preparation. His early coaches all rated him as just about the hardest-working, most enthusiastic player they had ever come across. He was one of a small group of Warrington players who called themselves The Wide Awake club. In addition to their usual demanding training schedule, they would meet up for 'extras' at 5.30 in the morning.

That sort of dedication brought its rewards: the Premiership in 1986, another Lancashire Cup in 1989, a try at Wembley in 1990, the captaincy of the Wire whilst still in his early 20s. He was one of the most popular players ever to wear the famous primrose and blue colours.

The same could be said of the red, white and blue. He scored two tries on his Great Britain debut against France at Headingley in 1987 and, the following year, was the only Warrington player on the Lions tour to Papua New Guinea, Australia and New Zealand, playing in all the Tests.

They included the unforgettable third game of the Australian series at the Sydney Football Stadium. The Ashes were already lost, the Lions were looking at a run of defeats stretching back ten years and, just for good measure, had a long list of injured players. Not surprisingly, they were given no chance whatsoever, even by the thousands of British supporters who had made the trip of a lifetime. That those fans came away with indelible memories of a rare GB triumph was largely down to Mike Gregory.

A mix and match British team had played above and beyond expectations from the start, but only led by four points with 18 minutes to play. 'But then came the moment for which I'll probably be best remembered,' as Mike put it when he recalled it in future years.

It was not unknown, or even all that unusual, for Great Britain to be in with a chance within sight of the finish line, only to fall agonisingly short. The Two Gregorys broke the mould in 1988 - for a few years at least.

The unrelated Wigan scrum-half, Andy, made a break

from deep in his own territory. Mike was on his shoulder and, suddenly, in the clear; that is if you ever were in the clear when pursued by Wayne Pearce, the supreme athlete of this era of Aussie domination. No less a finisher than Martin Offiah was the player trying to get into a position to support, but he was being held back by Wally Lewis.

What went through Mike Gregory's mind was: 'If I'm going to run all this way, I might as well score.' Score he did and the third Test was won by a convincing 26-12. It would have been the highlight of anybody's career, although he also went on to captain Great Britain in home and away Test series wins over the Kiwis.

There was also a down-side. His last four seasons with Warrington saw him play only 33 games, thanks to a succession of injuries, notably to his knee and Achilles. 'If I was a horse, they would have shot me,' he said in his testimonial brochure in 1993.

It was probably a mistake after that to sign for Salford, but they were persistent and he was persuaded to give it a go. It was the one part of his playing career he was uncomfortable with, feeling that he had not given value for money. It was not for want of trying. He played his last game in October 1995 and told his namesake, Andy, then the Salford coach, that he could not carry on.

By then, his ambitions lay in coaching and his first opportunity to get some experience under his belt came when Clive Griffiths approached him to help with the Wales squad in the 1995 World Cup. It doesn't sound like a particularly big job now, but it was then, because Wales still had big players - the likes of Jonathan Davies, John Devereux, Scott Gibbs, Allan Bateman and Paul Moriarty. There was a great occasion and a hard-won victory over Western Samoa in Swansea, plus a semi-final defeat by England, in which the

Welsh were by no means disgraced. The tournament as a whole did nothing to rid Gregory of the coaching bug. He had proved to himself that he could not only play the game, but also communicate it to others. The two do not always go together.

His first appointment at club level was as assistant to Shaun McRae at St Helens. Within a month, Saints were beating the Bradford Bulls at Wembley, an achievement Mike did not feel he had been there long enough to share in the fullest sense. No such reservations the following season, when the Cup was retained and Mike knew that he had made a major contribution. Apart from working with the first-team squad, he coached the U21s, helping with the development of players like Paul Wellens, Mike Bennett and Mark Edmondson.

At the end of his third season with Saints, however, there was a palace coup, a counter revolution at Knowsley Road. Saints had led the way in becoming a club run by a chief executive - David Howes, in their case - rather than a board of directors. Naturally, that left rather a lot of disgruntled past and present directors fulminating on the sidelines. The club's form did not have to deteriorate very much for them to strike back and restore the old regime. Howes, McRae and Gregory were all told that their contracts were not being renewed - a euphemism for the sack.

'All three of us moved down different pathways; David Howes went to the Leeds Rhinos, Shaun moved to the newly-formed club, Gateshead Thunder, who went straight into Super League, and me, I chose the glamour route and went as head coach to Swinton Lions,' Mike recalled.

He went after, but didn't get, the vacant job at Widnes and, just as he was beginning to think that maybe coaching wasn't for him and contemplating a complete career change

219

with the Fire Service or the Police, he had a phone call from the Swinton chairman, Malcolm White. He took the job with the struggling club on a part-time basis.

His most vivid memory of his two seasons there was also the most painful - a 106-10 Challenge Cup thumping by a Leeds side including players of the calibre of Iestyn Harris, Keith Senior, Adrian Morley, Barrie McDermott and a very young Kevin Sinfield. At the end of his second season with the Lions, his contract was not renewed; the world of coaching was not exactly rolling out the red carpet for Mike Gregory. He found his way, however, through the medium of Academy rugby.

Greg had already had one stint as England Academy coach during his Swinton days, brought in by his great mate, the RFL's then performance director, Joe Lydon, in a case of what he called 'a bit of nepotism.' In two seasons in charge, he twice guided his side to series wins over France. On his return, after his sacking by Swinton, they won on tour to New Zealand, but lost both Tests to the crack Australian Schoolboys side.

The Aussies were due in Britain the following year and this time Gregory really set out his stall to beat them. After years of trying, the Poms finally succeeded in doing so, winning the two Tests 28-20 and 20-12 - the sort of margins where organisation and preparation can make all the difference.

Good players are crucial as well; Greg had a back-three in the forwards of Jon Wilkin, Gareth Hock and Jamie Langley to call upon, for instance. In the absence of an outstanding specialist hooker, Greg turned Bob Beswick, a back-rower at Wigan, into one. It was one of a number of decisions which made it apparent to observers that he knew what he was doing.

His stock was on the rise, even though some said that it wasn't the strongest Australian side. Mike was having none of that.

'If you look at the players who made it from that side into first grade in the NRL, there's Justin Poore, Ashton Simms, Keith Galloway, Jacob Lilyman, Ryan Hoffman, Tom Learoyd, Michael Weyman and Tim Smith to name but a few. So they can whinge as much as they like ... the bottom line was that they had come to win and had failed.'

Mike had a growing reputation as a coach who could get the best out of young players and set them on their way to successful careers. That was certainly true of many who passed through his hands in the Academy sides, with players like Danny McGuire, Rob Burrow, Luke Robinson and Kirk Yeaman all getting their first taste of representative rugby.

It was with that in mind that Wigan approached him in 2002 to work under Stuart Raper, with particular responsibility for coaching the U21s. He also worked with the first team and, in an odd little interlude, with Orrell, the local rugby union club that the Wigan owner, Dave Whelan, had acquired as part of his takeover of sport in the town. When Raper's assistant, John Kear, moved on to become head coach at Hull, Greg moved up into the gap that he left.

The messy sacking of Raper opened up another opportunity, as Mike was named as caretaker-coach, with Denis Betts as his number two. As can often happen in these situations, the form of the side under a supposedly temporary regime forced the club's hand. It probably wasn't Plan A, but Greg was popular with the fans and the media, and, most importantly, he was winning. There is a lot more to coaching than technical knowledge; for one thing, there is that indefinable quality that makes players want to run through a brick wall for you - and Mike Gregory had that in spades.

Although he was thrilled to get the chance to coach the team he supported as a boy, it was not an easy time to take the reins at Wigan. The club had been changing coaches, on average, every 18 months and the return of Maurice Lindsay had not revitalised them.

Greg thought he knew what was wrong; not a failure to sign the best young - and particularly local - talent, but a failure to hang onto it. The syndrome was familiar enough to anyone who watched Wigan. The latest kid would come into the first team and would be hailed, often by Maurice, as the greatest thing since sliced bread. Then he would have a couple of ordinary games, the way young players do, and suddenly he would be not good enough, never good enough, and flogged off and replaced by a more expensive, older player - often an Australian. It was a knee-jerk tendency Mike railed against when he was coaching the kids at the JJB and, when he became head coach, he was determined to reverse it.

'I am amazed to this day why the likes of Stephen Wild, Martin Aspinwall, Luke Robinson, Shaun Briscoe, Paul Johnson and David Hodgson, who all came through the youth system at Wigan, were allowed to leave the club,' he wrote. 'I feel it's criminal to allow home talent to leave.'

Mike knew that it wasn't quite as simple as that; some wanted to leave and some got so far off-side with the club that they had to go. Still, the fundamental philosophy was clear and it was one that resonated positively with the Wigan public. It was also successful, to an extent, as the Warriors lost in the Super League Grand Final in 2003 and the Challenge Cup final the following year. That latter near miss, however, came with clouds gathering around Mike's personal life.

At the start of 2003, just after he had been named assistant coach at Wigan, he took a Great Britain squad to the

World Sevens in Sydney. It was his belief that, whilst he was in Australia, he was bitten by a tick and infected with a disease called borrelia.

It was his wife, Erica, who spotted a rash on his bottom that is characteristic of the condition. Other symptoms included excessive fatigue, headaches and a twitching sensation in his right bicep, all of which he was inclined to put down to playing injuries. Then, during the build-up to the Grand Final, he collapsed on the team bus coming away from a press conference at Old Trafford.

People had already noticed a difference in him. He had always had what you might call a thick Wigan accent, which almost amounts to a slurring of words, if I can say that without offending every Wiganer, even among the completely healthy. In his case, his speech got gradually worse, leading some meeting him for the first time to assume that he was drunk or had suffered a stroke. He and Erica decided to tell the club about his situation, particularly their plan to go to America at the end of the season to see a specialist. That was the start of an increasingly bitter conflict between club and coach.

I won't go into the medical science - although I read plenty about it at the time - but, in a nutshell, Wigan believed he had Motor Neurone Disease and that he was not going to return to work; Dave Whelan had a relative who'd had the condition. Mike and Erica - a bio-chemist by training - stuck to the diagnosis of borrelia, nasty but curable, and Progressive Muscular Atrophy, nasty but not unstoppable, and believed he should be given the chance.

After an out-of-court settlement for wrongful dismissal further down the line, Mike encapsulated his feelings at that time. He was 'frozen out' by Wigan, he said. 'Never once did I feel that they were trying to aid my return to work. The continuing support of the fans and the players has made an horrific experience bearable.'

I'd kept in touch with Mike, notably to write a feature for *The Independent* about his feelings about his treatment by Wigan. It was after that appeared that the Gregorys approached me. It was the most flattering and the most daunting request I've ever had; he wanted his story to be told and he wanted me to tell it.

There are some things you can't refuse to do for someone. The trouble was that I just didn't have the time; if truth be told, I was already struggling, had I known it, with early symptoms of my own little difficulty. Also, I couldn't stomach the idea of making money from Mike's misfortune.

I was also fairly sure that it would lead me into conflict with Wigan, which was a lesser concern but one I didn't need. What we eventually agreed was that I would write the book, to be called *Biting Back*, but I would do it by remote control. Steve Manning would record and transcribe the lengthy interviews with Mike; I would knock it into shape. We soon had a publisher, Vertical Editions, and we set to work, Steve putting in the hard yards and me getting there when I could.

Sadly, that involved seeing a steady deterioration in Mike's condition. He remained determined to finish it, however, as something to hand down to his sons, Sam and Ben. After that, I waited for the backlash from Wigan, but it never came. My feeling about it now is that the club was not in an easy position, but it could have been handled much, much better.

I'm not particularly proud of *Biting Back* as a piece of sporting literature. The way we were working had its limitations and we had decided from the start that we would tell the story in a pretty straightforward, chronological way, which was not the way to do it if you wanted to sell books. Still, Mike and Erica felt it told their story and that was what mattered.

I learnt a lot from the process. I got to know the family, especially Mike's parents, Keith and Joan. I got to know a lot more about the nature of courage. I saw a different side of a number of people. Take Ellery Hanley, for instance; he has always treated me with relentless hostility, for no good cause as far as I could see. The other side showed when, at Wembley, he gave Mike his Challenge Cup medal. Alright, he had a few to spare, but as an almost mystical gesture of solidarity I know how much it meant to Mike.

Then there's Joe Lydon. I think Joe's image in rugby league, fairly or unfairly, is as a bit of a Goodtime Charlie. You couldn't have a more staunch mate, though, than he was to Mike. 'You often see people at their best in a situation like that,' he said. Countless former team-mates and opponents made their way to the family home at Standish Lower Ground. 'That was a sign of the respect in which he was held,' Joe says. I saw plenty come and go with a tear in the eye. The really humbling thing was the way Mike tried to jolly things along, still with a twinkle in his eye as he attempted to tell bad jokes. You could argue that the cruellest aspect of his illness was that it robbed such a superb athlete of the power of movement. If anything, though, the progressive loss of his voice was even crueller, because Mike loved a chat, a gossip, a spot of banter.

Mike Gregory died on 19 November 2007, at the ridiculously early age of 43. Not only was the church packed for the funeral, so were all the streets around as the service was relayed by loud-speaker. It was a heart-rending, emotional occasion, but it was far from being the end of his legacy.

I've long had a theory that he would have been England - or, even better, Great Britain - coach by now.

'I could certainly see that,' says Lydon. 'He would have been ideal. he was very patriotic, very full-on in everything he did. he was just a great lad to be around. I've no doubts that he would have gone on to bigger and better things. Players held him in such great esteem, whether it was with Great Britain or at Swinton.'

Nowhere is that more true than at Warrington, where memories of Mike take on concrete form.

Not only is there a Mike Gregory Suite in the main stand at the Halliwell Jones Stadium, but you can actually walk to the ground along Mike Gregory Way.

Joe Lydon is best qualified to reflect on what the man himself would have thought of that. 'Absolutely bizarre,' he says. 'It's not the sort of thing that would have occurred to us, all those years ago at Wigan St Pats.'

Some time later - I'm a little vague on the chronology - I phoned Erica. I didn't exactly say 'Great news, I've got Parkinson's Disease,' but there was one thing I wanted her to know. Whatever had gone wrong with me was not the result of any pressure I'd put myself under on their behalf. It was just part of a random, co-incidental illness which I was pre-programmed to get. It was enough, as Leonard Cohen said about his manager and former lover running off with all his money, to put a dent in my mood, but I knew, from watching Mike suffer, that mine is trivial by comparison.

As progressing muscular diseases go, I've got the good one. In that sense, Greg has continued to educate me even after his death. If ever I feel excessively sorry for myself, I think of him, propped up on pillows and struggling to communicate, and I reflect that what I have to put up with is nothing set alongside that.

I'm sure there were dark times - there must have been - but he remained astonishingly cheerful. As he said, we're all headed in the same direction, the only issue is the ... timing.

Mike is still much-missed and always will be, first of all by the family, which Erica, with her incredible strength, has held together magnificently, and after that by the concentric circles of friends, acquaintances and people who only saw him on the pitch or in the dug-out, or as an image on the television screen.

'I'll always miss him,' says Lydon. 'I wouldn't say I think about him every day, but there's certainly never a week goes by without me doing. If I've one regret - apart from the obvious one that he isn't around anymore - it's that my children never knew him as he was before the illness. That's the Mike Gregory I'll remember.'

I'll remember that one as well, but also the man who, although physically a shadow of his old self, showed the same determination as he faced and ultimately lost the biggest battle of his life.

If that isn't the stuff of inspiration, then I don't know what is.

● Dave Hadfield was the rugby league correspondent of *The Independent* for over 20 years - and may even still be. He is author or editor of nine books, including *Up and Over*, *Down & Under*, *XIII Winters*, *XIII Worlds*, *Learning Curve* and *Playing Away: Australians in British Rugby League*.

Afterword

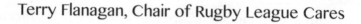

Terry Flanagan, Chair of Rugby League Cares

Rugby League Cares is rugby league's charity, established with the objective of unifying its existing charities - the Rugby League Foundation, the RFL Museums and Heritage Trust, and RFL Benevolent Fund - while also acting as the umbrella organisation for the professional clubs' charitable Foundations.

The vision is simple: working together will create and deliver more support for the sport and its people.

Our work focuses on four good causes supporting the past, present and future of rugby league: Grants, Welfare, Heritage and Benevolent Fund.

RL Cares was formed in August 2012 and since then we have gone on to achieve a great deal.

We have funded 70-plus grassroots projects, enabling each project to get started and provide opportunities for people to play and benefit from rugby league.

We've helped over 100 professional players with the provision of a small grant, designed to encourage them to undertake an educational course, which ultimately helps them to begin a new career after rugby. We are now seeing the first of those players leave the sport and start new occupations as a result of our help.

We are supporting former players by bringing them

together with old friends and team-mates under our project RL Cares Reunions. This work allows us to provide assistance to a growing number of individual welfare cases involving former players who are suffering through hardship, illness and poor health.

We've secured a number of grants which have enabled us to provide funding for State of Mind, launch a new dance project following the success of the dance during the 2013 RL World Cup and finally safeguard Mike Stephenson's heritage collection that was on display at the George Hotel.

None of the above would have been possible without the outstanding support we continually receive from the sport and its people. Rugby league is a sport that cares, as shown very clearly by the stories in these pages. This caring spirit is especially prominent in the face of tragedy.

Such support was also on display during the creation of this book and to all those who helped with its creation, we thank you. Our gratitude also goes to you, the reader, for purchasing your copy. We hope you enjoyed reading about some of the great deeds and actions of some truly remarkable people. The hope is that it will become the first of many. To that end, we know there are many inspirational figures who could have had their own chapter but haven't. If you have a candidate, let us know. Perhaps they will be in volume two.

I'll leave you with one final thought. If you liked this book and would like to get more involved in our work you can, by becoming a member of our organisation. Simply visit our website www.rugbyleaguecares.org. You will be making a huge difference to what we are doing right now and to the lives of those who need our help in the future.

Terry Flanagan, November 2014

Follow Rugby League Cares on Twitter: @RLCares

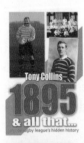
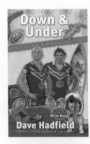

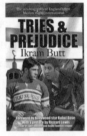

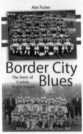
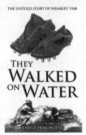

Strike!

The Tour That Died of Shame

By John Coffey

The 1926-27 New Zealand 'All Blacks' tour of Great Britain was the most tempestuous sporting venture of all time. It led to seven of the players being disqualified for life on their return home.

Set against the backdrop of a financially crippling miners' strike, the 'guilty' tourists rebelled against their controversial coach, an Australian who himself was suspended for part of the tour by English authorities.

Nineteen loyal players were left to carry on bravely against overwhelming odds in the midst of a harsh English winter, some of them backing up for as many as fifteen consecutive matches.

Strike! The Tour That Died of Shame is that story.

It is a tale of hardship and heroism, courage and cover-up, examined in depth for the very first time. It is an investigation of what went wrong with a tour that promised so much. It seeks to establish who - if anyone - was really to blame. And it is a fascinating slice of sporting social history whose reverberations continue to be felt today.

www.scratchingshedpublishing.com

"Schools rugby league is the lifeblood of the game..." Neil Fox MBE

DIFFERENT CLASS

The Story of Schools Rugby League

Around the turn of the 20th century, schools rugby league was formalised. Compiled from a nationwide archive, *Different Class* puts a long and illustrious history in context, capturing its flavour with an array of colourful contributions.

Examining the communities from which it sprang, neighbourhood rivalries, prevailing social conditions, stories of overcoming great odds and trips into the unknown, it traces the pioneering spirit that has characterised the schools game, and the role played by teachers as mentors and inspiring personalities. Mixing fact and anecdote, the book contains a wealth of reminiscences from some who went on to become superstars of the sport, alongside those for whom the school playing field was their zenith.

DIFFERENT CLASS

The Story of Schools Rugby League

Phil Caplan • Ron England

Phil Caplan ● Ron England

www.scratchingshedpublishing.com

Available now from Scratching Shed

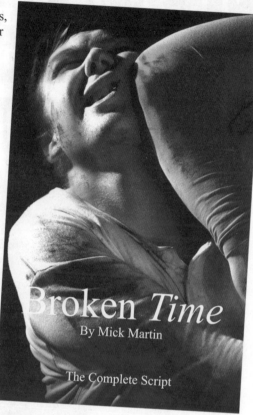

Curtain up on Lewy Jenkins, a young Welsh rugby player lured north by the promise of money and sporting glory; the David Beckham of his day. Lewy's sweetheart, Bessie Butterworth, is a rising star of the music hall. Beautiful and flirtatious, life has taught her harsh lessons.

These are the protagonists at the centre of *Broken Time*, a critically-acclaimed play by award-winning playwright Mick Martin. Set in Victorian Yorkshire, where fictional West Broughton Rugby Club are enduring a torrid run of defeats, it is a story of Corinthian idealism and class struggle amid the Industrial Revolution and tumultuous events that led to the historic rugby league - rugby union split of 1895.

After an eye-catching tour across the North of England, the complete script of *Broken Time* is published here for the first time. This edition also contains a foreword by Mick Martin himself and a specially commissioned introduction by respected rugby historian Professor Tony Collins.

Mick Martin's
Broken Time
- The Complete Script

Through Adversity is the story of Damian Clayton MBE, whose relentless pursuit of the rugby league dream has seen him brush shoulders with royalty, tour the world, receive a gong in 2008 and be voted Combined Services Sports Official of the Year.

Despite having long since achieved his main goal - to see rugby league recognised officially by the Armed Forces - the inspirational Royal Air Force Flight Sergeant continues to give his all to the sport he loves.

Clayton, the RAF's 'Mr Rugby League', has been on a long journey. Since 1992 he has worked tirelessly to ensure the sport he has graced as player, administrator and coach is given the same official recognition that dozens of other sports that military personnel take part in - such as football, cricket and tennis - take for granted.

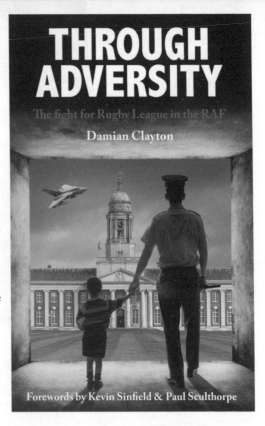

THROUGH ADVERSITY

The fight for Rugby League in the RAF

Damian Clayton

Forewords by Kevin Sinfield & Paul Sculthorpe

Through Adversity

By Damian Clayton MBE

Learning Curve

The Remarkable Story of Student League

Dave Hadfield

Learning Curve - Dave Hadfield's seventh book about rugby league - is devoted to one of the game's great untold stories.

The history of Student rugby league is marked by the defiance of prejudice and obstruction in building one of the code's most thriving sectors. Kicking off with the pioneers of the 1960s Hadfield traces the birth of the game in universities and colleges. From the founding fathers at Portsmouth and Leeds, he has gleaned the heroic truth behind those early years.

The spread of Student rugby league throughout England is highlighted by chapters on league development at Oxford and Cambridge - where sceptics said it would never penetrate.

From dozens of interviews with the most closely involved, alongside the author's inimitable observations of the state of play today, rugby league's best-loved writer captures the spirit of one of the sport's great successes - from the dedication at the elite level to humour in the lower echelons. Whether you played at university or college or not, *Learning Curve* is an unmissable read for those interested in the future of rugby.

DAVE HADFIELD

LEARNING CURVE

The Remarkable Story of Student Rugby League

■ Foreword by Brian Carney

www.scratchingshedpublishing.com

Investigate all our other titles and
stay up to date with our latest releases at
www.scratchingshedpublishing.co.uk